ALL IN
THE SAME BOAT

· · · · · · · · · · · · · ·

THE HUMORISTS'
GUIDE TO THE
OCEAN CRUISE

Other Humorists' Guides

Savoir Rire: The Humorists' Guide to France

COMING SOON:

Humorists' Guides to Italy, the British Isles, and the United States

ALL IN THE SAME BOAT

· · · · · · · · · · · · · ·

THE HUMORISTS' GUIDE TO THE OCEAN CRUISE

Edited by Robert Wechsler

Foreword by John Maxtone-Graham

CATBIRD PRESS

CATBIRD PRESS
44 North Sixth Avenue
Highland Park, NJ 08904
201-572-0816

Distributed to the trade by Independent Publishers Group

Printed and bound in the United States

The publisher wishes to acknowledge permission to include in this book copyright material as follows:

FRANKLIN P. ADAMS: "A Not Too Deep Sea Chantey" from *So There,* copyright 1923 by Doubleday, a division of Bantam, Doubleday, Dell Publishing Group, Inc. Reprinted by permission of the publisher. C. W. ANDERSON: Drawing by C. W. Anderson; © 1933, 1961 The New Yorker Magazine, Inc. ACKNOWLEDGMENTS are continued at the back of the book.

Library of Congress Cataloging-in-Publication Data

All in the same boat : the humorists' guide to the ocean cruise / edited by
  Robert Wechsler.
       p.   cm.
    ISBN 0-945774-01-X (pbk.) : $9.95
    1. Ocean travel — Humor.   2. Cruise ships — Humor.   I. Wechsler, Robert,
  1954-
  PN6231.O27A45   1988
  910.4'5'0207 — dc19   88-15973   CIP

CONTENTS

FOREWORD

SINCE I enjoy a laugh almost as much as shipboard,
this endearing volume compiled by Robert Wechsler
appeals to me on both counts. He has assembled
an entertaining, sometimes hilarious and always
fascinating compendium of passenger observations,
from years past to present. Passengers, especially
literate ones, make far better ocean liner critics than
naval architects or marine historians: they are there, on
the cutting edge of a storm and the duller edge of an
interminable crossing, a fractious shipmate or merely
an uncomfortable bunk. H. L. Mencken reminded me
how "the electric fan, when a stray zephyr blows in
through the porthole, makes a noise like a dentist drill."
   Thank heaven that editor Wechsler has thought to
include not only Somerset Maugham's "Mr Know-All"
in its entirety (perhaps the most evocative passenger
story of all time) but also dozens of snippets of
shipboard prose and poetry new to me. Browsing
through this book is like unpacking a steamer trunk of
long-forgotten delights and new treasures. It should be
sold on board all of today's cruise ships and sent as an
obligatory bon voyage present to everyone who sails
anywhere. "A stray zephyr" to cherish — it belongs in
every passenger's cabin and library.

                    JOHN MAXTONE-GRAHAM

R.M.S.MAURETANIA.LiquorDealersCruise.1960.

INTRODUCTION

TRAVEL guides are what you read when you want to know which cruise line to pick and what to see and when to go and what to do about such things as packing, booking a cabin, and getting through customs. This is not that sort of guide.

Humorists know that no matter which line you choose and what time you go, the same sorts of people will be your fellow passengers. Perhaps a little older or younger, richer or poorer, but they'll still be eating when you're full, running when you're exhausted, and grabbing up the guy or girl you had your eyes on. The humorist is sure that, whatever islands you stop at or fjords you enter, somehow you'll get lost on shore, and that when you finally get back to the ship, you'll be the only one who didn't buy this trinket or that. And he hopes you're proud, but not too boastful.

So forget everything you've ever thought about guidebooks. The advice here is much simpler: relax and enjoy. Remember, it's your vacation — holiday time — so don't annoy yourself about the size of the cabins or the skills of the stewards or the sharks. Well, if you have to worry about something, go ahead and worry about the sharks. Just bring along some raw meat so they'll be well fed.

The major difference between this guide and the other ones is that while the other guides focus on the inanimate — the accommodations, the sights, the menus — this guide focuses on the animate — the passengers, the stewards, the fish. Although we go on a cruise to get away from it all, we can't help but get into the thick of things, fortunately different and usually pleasant things, popularly known as people. Humor is not about *what* services await us on board, but *who* will manage not to provide them. It is interested not in where we set down our bags, but in the baggage we carry with us: awe and delight, playfulness and absurdity, dreams and nightmares, myths and stereotypes, platitudes and pretensions, expectations and obsessions, fear and anger and love.

Though The Humorists' Guides mainly concern themselves with countries, we chose the ocean cruise because it is the one form of transportation that is a destination in itself. Most passengers (and some cruise lines) now pick a goal merely to be able to tell their friends (or passengers) they're going *somewhere*.

Also, the ocean cruise has a long, some would say turbulent, history. It is as close as most of us will ever get to being characters out of the romantic novels and movies of our youth. The cruise ship stops at exotic lands; it travels on Neptune's unruly domain; it takes us out where there are actually stars and sunsets, and no newspapers.

Less romantically, an ocean cruise is like going back to camp or college, like starting all over with a whole new bunch of kids we don't have to spend all summer or four years with. They don't know you and your faults; you don't know them and theirs. What more can anyone ask?

Most important of all, the ocean cruise is a form of transportation many of our best humorists have taken. And what they take, they take on. If cruise lines had kept humorists from stowing away on board their ships, this book would not have been possible. So thank your cruise line for being such a sport.

Yes, *All in the Same Boat* is more than just another pretty guidebook. Behind that sparkling veneer is a serious humor anthology. Among the selections are many that are simply fun or silly or nonsensical, many that make unusual or ironic observations, many that tell stories, many that satire or parody or find some other way to poke fun at, many that take delight in what they see, for better or for worse, and some that do all of these at once. There are unknown finds, such as Frank Sullivan's ultimate cruise parody, "Captain's Dinner," as well as classics of the genre, such as the travel writing of Mark Twain. There is poetry by such poets as Lord Byron, Rudyard Kipling, and Oliver Wendell Holmes, Sr., which waxes eloquent, only to be brought abruptly back to earth, or sea. And then there are poems that examine such typically poetic subjects as seasickness, mothers-in-law, cruise captains, and jellyfish.

Many of the greatest English-speaking humorists and cartoonists are represented in these pages, some of them long out-of-print, but not forgotten. Americans will recognize the names of Mark Twain, Robert Benchley, S. J. Perelman, James Thurber, Clarence Day, Benjamin Franklin, Ogden Nash, Phyllis McGinley, H. L. Mencken, Will Rogers, Jean Kerr, Finley Peter Dunne, and John Updike. Britons will recognize the names of countrymen Lewis Carroll, Somerset Maugham, Sir Owen Seaman, Richard Gordon, Leigh Hunt, Stanley Ross, and R. G. G. Price. But less known today everywhere are such excellent humorists as, chronologically, John Phoenix (George H. Derby), Petroleum V. Nasby (David R. Locke), George Peck, Bill Nye, Arthur Guiterman, Irvin S. Cobb, Franklin P. Adams, Christopher Morley, Frank Sullivan, Donald Moffat, Wolcott Gibbs, Corey Ford, Margaret Fishback, Michael Musmanno, Lawrence Lariar, D. Keith Mano, and Nicholas Coleridge.

All in the Same Boat also includes selections from the work of travel writers with a sense of humor, many of whom are well known for their other works, particularly novels. People like Charles Dickens, William Dean Howells, Harriet Beecher Stowe, Lafcadio Hearn, Julia Ward Howe, E. W. Howe, and Stephen Longstreet.

And we can't forget the cartoonists and illustrators. Few of them are household names (except for Rube Goldberg and his machines), but few humorists or humor magazines would be the same without them. People like Gluyas Williams, Peter Arno, Herb Roth, Anatol Kovarsky, James Thurber, Ludwig Bemelmans, Mark Kelley, C. W. Anderson, and just a few of the cartoonists who have made *Punch* a British national institution on a par with the umbrella (and just as liable to turn inside out): Merrily Harpur, S. McMurtry, Donegan, and Henning Gentriis.

Well, that's enough names. At least now you won't have to bother with the table of contents. Enjoy, and let me thank all the people who have helped make *All in the Same Boat* possible, particularly the all-too-forgotten souls (are they humorists?!) who work in the permissions departments of publishing houses; the literary agents; the families of the humorists; and, most of all, those humorists themselves who have begrudgingly stuck around to force upon us more of their fun. Special thanks go to Mircea Vasiliu, whose work graces the cover; to Len Ringel, who designed everything you're looking at; and to any reader who gives another copy of this book as a present and thereby keeps the poor little Catbird in seed.

❧Preparations

❧*Like most things in life, an ocean cruise begins long before it begins, and it ain't over till you're over. From the moment of its conception, through the first argument (Ya think it's just like* Love Boat, *don't ya, you're just going for the girls. — Love Boat! Ha! I'm going with* you.*), and then the second argument, over where to go (the Caribbean, the Mediterranean, Alaska, the Galapagos, perhaps?), the cruise takes control of your life, much like a baby in the womb. You dream about it, you anticipate it, you long so for that time of pure relaxation that you can't bear to get up and go to work. And then, out of nowhere, comes dread: thoughts of whether your sea legs have gone the way of crab legs, doubts about your ability to bear the silence of the sea or the merriment of a floating dormitory. Sometimes these fears can gang up on you and threaten to change your mind, as with Keith Waterhouse in his response to former British Poet Laureate John Masefield's classic poem, "Sea Fever," which begins, "I must down to the seas again."*

Keith Waterhouse
Must I Go Down to
the Sea Again? 1967

Q4 OR NO Q4, you won't get me in one of those things. My fear of the sea is even more paralytic than my fear of flying, and I speak as one who can be got into the air only on the understanding that BOAC takes good care to get you smashed off your head. Fear is of course largely based on ignorance, and my ignorance of maritime matters goes full five fathoms deep, however deep that may be.

Ignorance of nomenclature. Do not know what fo'c'sle is, or what it has done to deserve more than its fair share of apostrophes. Do not know difference between starboard and portside. Do not know aft from elbow. Still have traumatic memory of writing battleship film

5

in which was put in humiliating situation of having to write: "The Captain comes downstairs and walks to the front of the ship."

Haziness about how to get on boat. Air travel simple in that one goes to airport, checks in and gets plastic boarding card. Do not know how to get on boat. Presumably must go to Southampton or Cherbourg or somewhere. Know that there are things called boat trains. Believe Golden Arrow drives straight on to ship. Is this case with Queen Mary? If so, why gangplanks? Hazy idea of big sheds — where pick up plastic boarding card?

Fear of being invited to Captain's Table. Would not know what to talk about, once weather and quality of Cordon Bleu glazed fish disposed of. Could tell Captain how Mark Twain got his name, but possibly he has heard story. Could ask him what think of works of W.W. Jacobs. Politics presumably barred; ladies' names not bandied in mess. No newspapers. So what talk about? "A friend of mine used to be in the navy." Oh, God.

Mistrust of naval vocabulary. Am assured that old and trusted phrases such as "All ashore that's going ashore," "Full steam ahead," "Women and children first" etc. still in use. Cannot possibly be associated with floating dictionary of clichés. While on this subject, what hope for decimal system when expressions like "eight bells" still used?

Dislike of sea sports. Am told that normal, sober businessmen, who on Transatlantic flights would not give one time of day, spend all waking hours afloat organising deck tennis, quoits, obscure bets on number of knots travelled etc. How far is knot? Is it same as nautical mile? Also, do we cross Equator on way to New York? Believe likelihood of hideous ceremony with self likely to be dressed up as Neptune.

Fear of funerals. Believe passengers who die from surfeit of Cordon Bleu glazed fish are buried at sea with Union Jack over them, with assembled passengers singing "For Those In Peril On The Sea." Do not know words. Would not know how to duck out of ceremony. Would have strange fear of wandering into hold or whatever where they keep spare coffins. While on this subject:

Fear of drowning. What if went for dip after Cordon Bleu glazed fish and drowned in swimming pool? Does this count as being lost at sea? Believe friends would laugh, like Graham Greene man who died when pig fell on head.

Ignorance of tipping procedure. Led to understand that everyone on ship expects large tip. Presumably this does not include Captain, but what about Bo'sun? What hell does Bo'sun do? Why not Bo's'un, like fo'c'sle? Assume on safe ground if tip only men in white coats, but what about tropics when officers wear white coats? "Waterhouse? Yes, he shipped into Singapore with us in '67. Tried to slip the First Officer a florin."

Antipathy towards lifeboat drill. Can never understand air hostess explaining how to get into simple life-jacket — tie round back, pull black knob etc. How can be expected to master complicated procedure of getting tarpaulin off lifeboat, lowering it to deck, finding salt tablets etc.? Believe this drill compulsory. Perhaps *viva voce* examination by First Mate: define difference between aft and starboard. Oh, God.

Uncertainness about people's titles. Know that there is bo'sun, purser etc. Could keep out of their way. Understand also that all waiters are called stewards, but could run into difficulties. "Steward, there's a fly in my Cordon Bleu glazed fish" sounds OK, but "If that's your attitude, ask the Head Steward to step this way" does not. Is head waiter same as chief steward?

Uncertainness about when to dress for dinner. Have read that formality is waived on first night out, but what constitutes first night out? Supposing board ship at night and it pulls up anchor or whatever it does first thing in morning? Was last night in dock first night out? Or is second night first night out? Oh, God.

Mistrust of shipboard romances. Have not read Somerset Maugham for nothing — know that only alternative to playing poker with cardsharpers is being pursued round and round deck by amorous widows. Something to do with throbbing of ship's engines. Captain authorised to solemnise weddings — fear of being involved in farcical ceremony reminiscent of Warner Brothers picture circa 1937.

Haziness about how to get off boat. Know how to get off aeroplane — shuffle after other passengers and say: "Thank you" to hostess. Get hat blown off on runway. How get off ship? Stand at front end looking at Statue of Liberty, but then what? Cornish vessel *Merry Dick,* after journey round Seal Island, puts passengers into little boats which drive them (row them) to St. Ives. Is this case with Queen Mary? What about luggage? Who purser? Does purser take luggage? Should one tip purser? Is luggage taken to big sheds? How get into big sheds off little boats? Oh, God.

Also, I get seasick.

Thomas R. Ybarra
The Landlubber's Toast 1908

'Tis pleasant to taste of the spray
As the waters dash over the rail
   To be frozen and wet
   And extremely upset
In the teeth of a thundering gale.
But the joys of a seafaring life
Are naught but the emptiest boast,
   As glasses we clink
   In a room that can't sink
   And delightedly drink
A new toast:
   "Oh, here's to the land, yo ho!
   Drain, drain every foaming tankard,
     Oh, here's to the sea
     As it looks to me
   From a beach that is firmly anchored.
     Oh, here's to the quiet, respectable street
     Where the winds never howl and the waves
       never beat,
     Where the ground has been trained to stick
       close to your feet, —
     A health to the land, yo ho!"

There's a charm in the mariner's life,
Of pleasure he suffers no lack,
   As he tumbles through space
   The winds slap his face
And the boom makes a dent in his back.
When the waves wash him over the side
In a playful and innocent style,
   The fishes who note
   His descent from the boat
   Eat him up, table d'hôte,
With a smile.
   "So here's to the land, yo ho!
   Drain, drain every tankard foaming;
     The delights I resign
     Of the billowy brine —
Let others do all my roaming.

Oh, here's to the land where you stick to your chairs,
Where the beds do not fire you out unawares,
Where you know which is down, and which is
    up-stairs —
A health to the land, yo ho!"

❧*Once you've overcome these silly feelings, which bear absolutely no relation to reality and will, if you let on to anyone, ruin your well-earned reputation for sanity and clearheadedness, the first thing you have to do is book passage. Now that the big decisions are over — going at all and where — you've got to make all the little, really tough ones, like cruise line, date, class, cabin placement, and theme (music, baseball players, singles, doubles, triples). Here's classic American novelist William Dean Howells' experience.*

William Dean Howells
We'll Take It *1899*

FROM this time their decision to go was none the less explicit because so perfectly tacit.

They began to amass maps and guides. She got a Baedeker for Austria and he got a Bradshaw for the continent, which was never of the least use there, but was for the present a mine of unavailable information. He got a phrase-book, too, and tried to rub up his German. He used to read German, when he was a boy, with a young enthusiasm for its romantic poetry, and now, for the sake of Schiller and Uhland and Heine, he held imaginary conversations with a barber, a bootmaker, and a banker, and tried to taste the joy which he had not known in the language of those poets for a whole generation. He perceived, of course, that unless the barber, the bootmaker, and the banker answered him in terms which the author of the phrase-book directed them to use, he should not get on with them beyond his first question; but he did not allow this to spoil his pleasure in it. In fact, it was with a tender emotion that he realized how little the world, which had changed in everything else so greatly, had changed in its ideal of a phrase-book.

Mrs. March postponed the study of her Baedeker to the time and place for it, and addressed herself to the immediate business of ascertaining the respective merits of the *Colmannia* and *Norumbia*. She carried on her researches solely among persons of her own sex; its experiences were alone of that positive character which brings con-viction, and she valued them equally at first or second hand. She heard of ladies who would not cross in any boat but the *Colmannia,* and who waited for months to get a room on her; she talked with ladies who said that nothing would induce them to cross in her. There were ladies who said she had twice the motion that the *Norumbia* had, and the vibration from her twin screws was fright-ful; it always was, on those twin-screw boats, and it did not affect their testimony with Mrs. March that the *Norumbia* was a twin-screw boat too. It was repeated to her in the third or fourth degree of hearsay that the discipline on the *Colmannia* was as perfect as on the Cunarders; ladies whose friends had tried every line assured her that the table of the *Norumbia* was almost as good as the table of the French boats. To the best of the belief of lady witnesses still living who had friends on board, the *Colmannia* had once got aground, and the *Norumbia* had once had her bridge carried off by a tidal wave; or it might be the *Colmannia;* they promised to ask and let her know. Their lightest word availed with her against the most solemn assurances of their husbands, fathers, or brothers, who might be all very well on land, but in navigation were not to be trusted; they would say anything from a reckless and culpable optimism. She obliged March all the same to ask among them, but she recognized their guilty insincerity when he came home saying that one man had told him you could have played croquet on the deck of the *Colman-nia* the whole way over when he crossed, and another that he never saw the racks on in three passages he had made in the *Norumbia.*

The weight of evidence was, he thought, in favor of the *Norum-bia,* but when they went another Sunday to Hoboken, and saw the ship, Mrs. March liked her so much less than the *Colmannia* that she could hardly wait for Monday to come; she felt sure all the good rooms on the *Colmannia* would be gone before they could engage one.

From a consensus of the nerves of all the ladies left in town so late in the season, she knew that the only place on any steamer where your room ought to be was probably just where they could not get it. If you went too high, you felt the rolling terribly, and people tramp-ing up and down the promenade under your window kept you awake the whole night; if you went too low, you felt the engine thump, thump, thump in your head the whole way over. If you went too far forward, you got the pitching; if you went aft, on the kitchen side, you got the smell of the cooking. The only place, really, was just back of the dining-saloon on the south side of the ship; it was smooth there, and it was quiet, and you had the sun in your window all the way over. He asked her if he must take their room there or nowhere, and she answered that he must do his best, but that she would not be satisfied with any other place.

In his despair he went down to the steamer office, and took a room which one of the clerks said was the best. When he got home, it appeared from reference to the ship's plan that it was the very room his wife had wanted from the beginning, and she praised him as if he had used a wisdom beyond his sex in getting it.

He was in the enjoyment of his unmerited honor when a belated lady came with her husband for an evening call, before going into the country. At sight of the plans of steamers on the Marches' table, she expressed the greatest wonder and delight that they were going to Europe. They had supposed everybody knew it, by this time, but she had not heard a word of it; and she went on with some felicitations which March found rather unduly filial. In getting a little past the prime of life he did not like to be used with too great consideration of his years, and he did not think that he and his wife were so old that they need be treated as if they were going on a golden wedding journey, and heaped with all sorts of impertinent prophecies of their enjoying it *so* much and being *so* much the better for the little outing! Under his breath, he confounded this lady for her impudence; but he schooled himself to let her rejoice at their going on a Hanseatic boat, because the Germans were always so *careful* of you. She made her husband agree with her, and it came out that he had crossed several times on both the *Colmannia* and the *Norumbia*. He volunteered to say that the *Colmannia* was a capital sea-boat; she did not have her nose under water all the time; she was steady as a rock; and the captain and the kitchen were simply out of sight; some people did call her unlucky.

"Unlucky?" Mrs. March echoed, faintly. "Why do they call her unlucky?"

"Oh, I don't know. People will say anything about any boat. You know she broke her shaft, once, and once she got caught in the ice."

Mrs. March joined him in deriding the superstition of people, and she parted gayly with this over-good young couple. As soon as they were gone, March knew that she would say: "You must change that ticket, my dear. We will go in the *Norumbia*."

"Suppose I can't get as good a room on the *Norumbia*?"

"Then we must stay."

In the morning after a night so bad that it was worse than no night at all, she said she would go to the steamship's office with him and question them up about the *Colmannia*. The people there had never heard she was called an unlucky boat; they knew of nothing disastrous in her history. They were so frank and so full in their denials, and so kindly patient of Mrs. March's anxieties, that he saw every word was carrying conviction of their insincerity to her. At the end she asked what rooms were left on the *Norumbia,* and the clerk whom they had fallen to looked through his passenger list with a shaking head. He was afraid there was nothing they would like.

"But we would take *anything,*" she entreated, and March smiled to think of his innocence in supposing for a moment that she had ever dreamed of not going.

"We merely want the best," he put in. "One flight up, no noise or dust, with sun in all the windows, and a place for fire on rainy days."

They must be used to a good deal of American joking which they do not understand, in the foreign steamship offices. The clerk turned unsmilingly to one of his superiors and asked him some question in German which March could not catch, perhaps because it formed no part of a conversation with a barber, a bootmaker, or a banker. A brief drama followed, and then the clerk pointed to a room on the plan of the *Norumbia* and said it had just been given up, and they could have it if they would decide to take it at once.

They looked, and it was in the very place of their room on the *Colmannia;* it was within one of being the same number. It was so providential, if it was providential at all, that they were both humbly silent a moment; even Mrs. March was silent. In this supreme moment she would not prompt her husband by a word, a glance, and it was from his own free will that he said, "We will take it."

&*Now that you have your berth, it's time to tell your friends and family. Tell them early and often enough so that they'll plan a bon-voyage party or go to see you off, or both. Flying somewhere may be ho-hum these days when nearly everyone seems to be a jet-setter, but taking a cruise still retains that exotic aura. After all, only travel on a ship is truly a voyage. It's certainly more than enough of an excuse for people to give you that party you deserve, or for you to give them the party they deserve (featuring just desserts). But before you get on the phone to the worst caterer in town, listen to the advice of the well-traveled Robert Benchley and the mal-voyage wishes of that most well-traveled and prolific author of them all, Anonymous.*

Robert Benchley
Seeing-Off *1930*

I AM sailing for Europe shortly and I would like to take this way of announcing to my hundreds, nay dozens, of friends that I can do without a farewell party on sailing-night. The week before — O.K. But not on the night of sailing. I simply have *got* to sail this time.

In the first place, I am on the wagon and would just be a death's head at the feast. But it has been my experience that, drinking or not, the person who is departing, and in whose honor the ice-cream and cookies are being served, is likely to be something of a death's head anyway. He has too much on his mind.

There is the packing to be thought of. If he is any kind of person at all he has left his packing until that night. This more or less begins to prey on his mind along about nine o'clock. There is no sense in being an old woman about getting packed ahead of time, but if the ship sails at midnight, at least he ought to begin getting his bags out of the hall-closet by nine and lining them up on the floor. The thought that he hasn't done even this, while it doesn't actually drive him from the party, prevents his entering whole-heartedly into the party spirit. Somewhere in the back of his brain is that little imp who keeps tap-tap-tapping and saying, "Come, come, lazy-bones! You don't even know whether your bags are *in* the hall-closet or not." And this sort of thing puts a damper on fun-making. Even if the guest-of-honor has been drinking fulsome toasts to himself all evening, they have no effect on him other than to impede digestion. And if, as I shall be, he is on the wagon, then a more miserable man could not be found in all the countryside 'round.

But above all things he must not tell his friends that he is not yet packed. This news would at once start a huzza and a frenzied dash on the part of all present to "help good old Bob pack!" "Everybody up to Bobby's and get him packed!" This is fatal. I once sailed, after being assisted by willing hands, with a suitcase entirely filled with telephone-directories (Westchester and Long Island, with a Brooklyn and Queens tucked in to keep the others from rattling about) and a hatbox containing damp sand in which various species of crustaceans were thriving. Dear, *dear* friends! How I shall miss them this year! That is, if I have anything to say about it.

These farewell parties, although they are conceived in what is ostensibly a spirit of friendliness toward the traveler, usually develop a subtle antagonism toward him as the evening wears on. Instead of being the hero of the occasion he gradually becomes the patsy and everything possible is done to confuse and chagrin him. He tries to enter into the spirit of the thing, but the gesture is a weak one, and easy-going as he may be, the thought of the ride, possibly to Hoboken, which lies ahead of him, to say nothing of the little odds and ends which still remain to be done (such as getting his passport photographs taken) makes his *esprit* a rather ghastly mockery. Along about ten he looks at his watch more frequently, a tactical error which brings down a storm of ridicule from his friends.

"Oh, *you've* got time enough!" they scream. "Don't you worry! *We'll* get you on the ship all right, if we have to buy it and hold it for you — won't we, boys?" And a collection is started to buy the ship and hold it until the next morning.

At about ten-thirty the victim of the entertainment, his mind as clear as a bell, realizes that he has not only to go home and pack and drive to the pier (the ship I am planning to take sails from just off Fort Hamilton, from which the light on Bishop's Rock, England, can be seen on a clear night) but that he also has to manage a good-natured crowd of merry-makers, many of whom have already started to kiss him good-bye. It is a fairly staggering prospect.

Even if he does succeed in breaking away and getting his bags packed (a supposition too silly even to consider) he has to look forward to the horror of getting on board accompanied by his little playmates. After all, he has got to stay on the ship for six days and would like to be on at least easy enough terms with the rest of the passengers so that they would not draw their feet up onto their deck-chairs as he walks past. But, as his well-wishers swarm over the sides of the ship, bowling old gentlemen over and violating the privacy of cabins adjacent to his, he realizes that the best thing for him to do will be to keep to his berth for the first three days and have his meals brought in. Otherwise he will be pointed out among the ship's company as "that man."

There is no place where unseemly behavior shows up more vividly than in the crowd who have come down to see a ship off. Hundreds of people milling about, some crying softly in little groups, others crying loudly at stateroom doors, families breaking up, lovers saying good-bye, mothers bidding farewell to daughters, emotional French ladies in black, sobbing subjunctives on the shoulders of what seem to be stewardesses — and into this gathering of breaking hearts barges our hero, borne on the shoulders of his light-hearted well-wishers singing "Hinky-dinky-parlay-voo!" He tries to act as if he were not with them, but they will have none of it. Down to his cabin they go with him, pushing open stateroom doors as they go past, speaking to people they do not know, turning on the taps in his washstand, snapping the lights on and off and all piling into his bunk as a final evidence of *bonhomie*. The whole thing is very unfortunate.

He is lucky if he gets them all out of his room before the ship sails. Several may have to go off with the pilot. There is something terrifying about the unanimity with which all seeing-off parties decide to stay right there in the room and "sail with good old Benny." "We could get clothes from the steward," they say, "or even wear our evening-clothes all the way over." Considering the number of times this whimsical suggestion has been made, it gets a surprisingly big laugh at each offering. And, for a time, it looks as if they really meant to go through with it. Stewards come and plead in vain for them to go ashore. Horns blow, whistles moan, gongs bang, but all to no effect. "We've got plenty of time yet," seems to be the consensus of opinion. "They always blow those things an hour before they really sail." And there is another song and another toast drunk out of soap-dishes and another suggestion that they sail with good old Benny and wear their evening-clothes all the way across. The best way for the departing member to handle them is to say that he has decided not to sail after all, get off the boat and lure them with him. Then he can suddenly turn and run back after getting half way down the pier and, if he is lucky, be pulled in with the gangplank.

And that is why, my good friends, I would rather stumble, a solitary, sobbing figure, on board my ship when it sails, with no cheering words of good-bye, by no hearty handclasps of friendship, no memory of affectionate toasts ringing in my ears. It is better so. I am a lonely man, and lonely will I put out to sea.

Anonymous
His Mother-in-Law

He stood on his head by the wild seashore,
    And danced on his hands a jig;
In all his emotions, as never before,
    A wildly hilarious grig.

And why? In that ship just crossing the bay
    His mother-in-law had sailed
For a tropical country far away,

Where tigers and fever prevailed.

Oh, now he might hope for a peaceful life
    And even be happy yet,
Though owning no end of neuralgic wife,
    And up to his collar in debt.

He had borne the old lady through thick and thin,
    And she lectured him out of breath;
And now as he looked at the ship she was in
    He howled for her violent death.

He watched as the good ship cut the sea,
    And bumpishly up-and-downed,
And thought if already she qualmish might be,
    He'd consider his happiness crowned.

He watched till beneath the horizon's edge
    The ship was passing from view;
And he sprang to the top of a rocky ledge
    And pranced like a kangaroo.

He watched till the vessel became a speck
    That was lost in the wandering sea;
And then, at the risk of breaking his neck,
    Turned somersaults home to tea.

---

*Before you get started, there are some things you'll need to know.
For example, it's probably been a long, long time since you last read a
novel by C. S. Forester or Joseph Conrad, so your nautical vocabulary
might be rustier than the hull of your ship. For you landlubbers, here's
a little dictionary put together by travel humorist Lawrence Lariar.*

Lawrence Lariar
Nautical Dictionary 1956

BOW: The front of the boat.
AFT: The part behind the front.
STERN: The fat part behind the aft.
WAKE: The water behind the part behind the aft.
UP FORWARD: Any part of the ship in front of the stern.
AMIDSHIPS: The section of the ship in front of the stern and right
    behind the bow.

DOWN BELOW: The stuff directly beneath any of these parts.

PORT: The left side of the ship. Seasoned travelers will look down their noses at you unless you use this nautical term. Instead of saying: *"I saw that hussy kissing your husband on the left side of the boat,"* you should say: *"I saw that hussy kissing your husband PORT SIDE."* On the other hand, it may be better to keep your mouth shut about what you saw.

STARBOARD: The right side of the vessel. Nautical experts disagree about the derivation of this term. Some say it comes from an old Scandinavian word: *"Stryvgbrynnd!,"* which means *"A herring that always swims to the right."* Others say it was created to sound just as meaningless as *"port,"* which is probably closer to the truth.

COMPANIONWAY: A narrow stairway for sitting with your companion, provided she's skinny enough. Fatter companions may be seated on your lap.

SALOON: (Sometimes called *"salon," "lounge"* or just plain *"lobby."*) A large, plush room where first-class passengers get together with other first-class passengers for purposes of exchanging strictly second-class dialogue.

BAR: A smaller room down below where the poorer passengers drink too many highballs and will talk to anybody in sight.

COCKTAIL LOUNGE: Another room with softer chairs, dim lights and tender music, usually filled by sleepy alcoholic passengers who are usually filled.

SHIP'S POOL: A maritime betting game designed to satisfy all the bookies, touts and horse players on the passenger list. The method of play is simple. Everybody guesses the number of miles the ship will cover in a day's run. Each bettor wagers on his guess, after which the seasoned travelers sit back and smirk at the guesses of the neophyte voyagers. (After which the pool is usually won by a little old lady who didn't know she was betting at all, but thought she was making a contribution to have the ship's swimming pool filled.)

J. ARTHUR SMERDLAP: The way a man yclept Jackson Smith has had his name spelled on the Passenger List.

PASSENGER LIST: A list of names published by the printing plant on the vessel to confound the passengers who are proud of their monikers. Typical typographical errors will include: Hiram Ookle (Hiram Ormsby), Etoin Shrdlu (Enid Smith), Lancaster Q. Balyworglish (Lester Jones), J. Foster Dullest (Sam Ginsburg), J. Edward Hoovering (Lowell Thomas).

SHUFFLEBOARD: A deck game that involves pushing little round slices of wood all over the place while waiting for the next meal to happen.

SEASICKNESS: A strange malady that attracts passengers to the rails where they stare open-mouthed at the sea.

MAL DE MER: The same malady on a French steamship.

STATEROOM: A large, commodious, well-decorated, well-ventilated room, convenient to the deck, containing a private shower and a wonderful view of the ocean, for which you paid your travel agent a huge sum of money.

CABIN: The small, stuffy, airless, showerless and hopeless closet you wound up with when you boarded the vessel.

ROOM STEWARD: A member of the ship's staff assigned to make you feel comfortable in your room throughout the voyage and up until the moment you hand him his tip, after which you feel like Scrooge.

DINING ROOM STEWARD, DECK STEWARD, BATH STEWARD: Three other flunkeys who can make you feel just as cheap as the Room Steward did.

FIRST CLASS: The part of the boat reserved for the very wealthy.

CABIN CLASS: The middle section of the boat, assigned to the middle-class people. Passengers in Cabin Class are invariably trying to sneak into First Class functions to hobnob with the elite. Passengers in First Class, however, can spot a Cabin Class bum instantly and have him put in his place (out) at once.

TOURIST CLASS: The passengers in the bottom part (bilge) of the ship. Most of these folks are much too poor to begin envying the people in First Class, but are just rich enough to loathe everybody in Cabin Class.

CUSTOMS: A ritual period after the ship docks, during which passengers are required to open their luggage for inspection by government agents who are searching for smuggled diamonds, dope, marihuana, Japanese beetles, dry rot, opium and other "undeclared" items. The entire procedure usually only takes about ten minutes, but consumes more than two hours *en toto* because of those slowpokes ahead of you.

DUTY: A tax levied by customs men against voyagers unlucky enough to be caught with their undeclared imports showing.

AVAST! A nautical way of saying: *"Stop!"* (For example: a young lady unacquainted with the language of the sea, when accosted by an amorous marine wolf, might say: *"Stop it, big boy, or I'll yell for help!"* Whereas, a girl familiar with nautical semantics would probably shout: *"Avast! Port your helm, matey, or I'll trim your yardarm!"*)

AS THOUSANDS CHEER

IN THIS interesting composition, the master has caught with characteristic *brio*, the verve, the *va et vient*, the *brouhaha* of a *Paris* sailing.

That elegant creature, footing it so featly up the gangplank, is the Duchess of Badminton. By landing at Plymouth, she'll save a day, and be at the Towers in time to open the Vicar's Bazaar for the St. Asaph's Junior Boys Club at Little Torkington-under-Tyne.

She's blowing kisses to the *Tout New York*, down to wish her *Bon Voyage*. Just a formality, of course . . .

all voyages are *bons*, on the *Paris* . . . and why shouldn't they be? The service, for instance . . . shall we say impeccable? And the food! Don't get us started on the food, unless you want to see us break out in a rash of superlatives. And as far as the Atlantic is concerned, it better not try any of its tricks on these Breton sailors. They won't stand for any nonsense from an ocean they've known since they were knee-high to a lobster.

Among those present . . . but you know all these people, don't you?

You run into them everywhere, on the *Paris*, in Who's Who, at Ascot, walking with a friend in the Bois. . . . Or in the office of your travel agent.

❧Departure

❧*Now you're ready to set sail, weigh anchor, shove off, or, simply, leave. The breeze feels good and, what with all the shouting and shoving and crying, you're excited and ready. But there you stand, as if at the end of the high dive or, more appropriately, at the end of the plank a pirate's making you walk. You want nothing but for it to get over with, for the passengers to be separated from their friends, for the quiet of the open sea, for the food and the games and the sweetly rocking motion to commence. You feel just like humorists Clarence Day, best known for his* Life with Father *books, and Margaret Fishback in the following farewell poems. But sometimes things don't work out the way you hope, as in the following excerpts from the humorous works of Corey Ford and Donald Moffat.*

Clarence Day
Farewell, My Friends *c1930*

> Farewell, my friends — farewell and hail!
> I'm off to seek the Holy Grail.
>   I cannot tell you why.
> Remember, please, when I am gone,
> 'Twas Aspiration led me on.
> Tiddlely-widdlely tootle-oo,
> All I want is to stay with you,
>   But here I go. Goodbye.

Margaret Fishback
All Ashore That's Going Ashore 1936

Farewell to apoplectic horn,
  To banshee brake and grinding gear,
To ash can, mating in the morn
  With roving truck. I shall not hear
The old concerto of distress
  For days! The 'phone, — it too will be
A whisper in the wilderness
  As I put out to sea.

Corey Ford
Too Many Goodbyes 1929

SAN FRANCISCO in 1839! A tangled mass of shipping in the harbor, tugs, ferries, and scurrying yachts, here and there a canoe filled with Indians trading wampum; before the log cabins on the hill a platoon of soldiers already drilling for the Civil War; and tied up to the quaint pier, her blue flag flying and her crew of hardy adventurers staring all unknowing for the last time at this scene of bustling activity, the ill-fated Kawa stood ready to embark upon what was to prove her final voyage.

Whistles were blowing, sirens shrieking, somewhere a steward's gong rang faintly and a bugle sounded its warning note. The crowd of friends on the dock waved their hats aloft in tearful farewell to the intrepid explorers, bound for none knew how long, alas! amongst the savage cannibals of the South Seas. 'So long, Swank!' they called. 'A good trip to you, Whinney!' and 'Farewell, Dr. Walter H. Traprock! Farewell to you!' came from the choking throats of the weeping relatives on the pier. My father stood beside the taffrail, staring at his watch. At precisely three minutes to three, always an ominous moment in the lives of sailor-folk, he nodded his head gravely, and the excited crew ran up the sails, ran down again sheepishly and stood on the deck instead, while the magnificent white wings of the doomed ship spread themselves slowly to the wind. The band of forty pieces struck up 'Valencia,' and Mother forced a tearful smile. A deadly foreboding that seems instinctive with the womenfolk of deep sea sailors had come upon her.

'They're off!' shouted the crowd on the dock. 'Remember me to the South Seas, Herman! Reginald, don't forget to write! Oh, *Wal*-ter! Goodby! Goodby!'

'Goodbye!' shouted the adventurers, a suspicious catch in their voices.

'Goodbye!' shouted the crowd on the shore again.

The Kawa's sails billowed and filled. Father grasped the wheel in anticipation. Mother swayed and fell to the pier in a dead faint.

'Goodby! Goodby!' cried Dr. Traprock, trying to smile.

'Goodby!' replied the crowd again; and for five or ten minutes they continued to wave hats and flags and shout 'Goodby!' now and then casting surreptitious glances at their watches. At the end of half an hour the band stopped playing 'Valencia,' and Mother came out of her faint and began to wave her handkerchief again.

'Well, we're off,' shouted Swank, to fill the embarrassing silence.

'Yeh?' replied the crowd a little suspiciously.

'Why don't you start then?' demanded a voice in the rear.

'Why *don't* we start!' Dr. Traprock whispered uneasily to Father.

Father only shook his head. For once he was baffled. The wind was with them, all the passengers were aboard, they had their clearance papers. In the meantime the crowd on the pier was thinning out perceptibly. The band had packed its forty pieces and walked over to a nearby trolley-car. Mother had fainted again, from sheer weariness. Poor Whinney tried to brighten the rapidly increasing gloom by tossing a roll of colored streamer to a friend on the dock. It missed the edge of the pier by several feet and sank limply into the water, where it slowly disappeared. The friend retaliated by tossing another roll of colored streamer at the ship, which failed to unroll in its flight and struck Swank smartly in the eye. There was an exchange of dirty looks.

'Ah, let's give her a push,' someone in the crowd laughed sourly.

'Well, why don't you go home?' demanded Whinney. 'You don't have to wait if you don't want to.'

'You're darned tootin' we don't,' the crowd replied, as they turned and walked away in disagreeable silence.

'I hope you *stay* home,' called Swank.

'I hope you stay in the South Sea,' retorted the last of the crowd over their shoulders. The hardy adventurers stared bitterly at the deserted pier. Father bit his lip in defeat. Dr. Traprock wandered disconsolately toward the stern.

'Captain,' he called presently, 'I've just been wondering if it would help to untie the Kawa from the dock?'

Donald Moffat
Nothing Happened 1937

THE purest case of *Système D* [making up rules as one goes along] I
ever saw was leaving Le Havre in the old *Talleyrand* once. Did I
ever tell you about that?"

"No," said Mr. Mott. This is Mr. Poulter's story: —

He stood leaning over the forward rail, high up on the boat deck
of the old *Talleyrand,* outward bound from Le Havre, and idly
looked down upon the familiar scenes of departure: parents herding
small, tired, but indomitable children; elderly ladies glaring at each
other as they tried to corner the deck steward to demand preferred
space for their chairs; the throng that always considers waving one
of the more thrilling ingredients of travel lining the rail and waving at
France in general; the inevitable drunks, unnecessarily prolonging
their farewell Paris parties; the theatrical blonde, making sure that
her departure from her native soil did not escape unnoticed, by
weeping, screaming with laughter, and kissing her hands repeatedly
to a stout and seedy-looking man in a frock coat on the dock below,
who failed to exhibit analogous symptoms of excitement and sorrow. Behind her prowled the ship's wolves, one by one, noncha-
lantly, watchfully, an anticipatory gleam in the eye, a knowing smile
on the lips of each. Mr. Poulter bet on a black one with a waxed
moustache.

The whistle blew, the gangway was lowered and slid out of sight
beneath the shed, the cables were slipped and splashed into the
water, the blonde redoubled the jocund frenzy of her adieus, and the
wavers waved as if they would never wave again. Once more the
whistle sounded. I guess we're off, thought Mr. Poulter.

But nothing happened. Mr. Poulter felt for the little preliminary
shiver of engines getting to work. There was no shiver. From his ele-
vation he could look down upon the bridge, where a group of officers on the starboard wing were gazing intently forward and down.
He followed their eyes, and saw that the ship was still fast by a forward cable. Two little bearded workmen in dirty caps, jumpers,
baggy overalls were wrestling with their end, on the dock.

The cable looked old and rusty. Apparently the bight had somehow become twisted, and was too small to slip over the head of the
bollard.

A young officer called down to the workmen through a megaphone, from the bridge. One of the old gentlemen knocked off long

enough to reply in triplicate, with gestures, while the other scratched his head. Presently the captain himself, who had been impatiently pacing the bridge, seized the megaphone and bellowed something else through it, which persuaded one of the navvies to stroll off into the shed, whence he soon returned with a crowbar. He pried; both pried. Nothing happened. The party was augmented by three strapping fellows — baggage porters, from their blue blouses — who seemed to consider it a most arresting problem from the point of view of theoretical physics. They were interested — not enough to throw their muscles into the balance, but sufficiently to lend copious advice. The captain roared again, and pointed, fiercely. The biggest porter shouted back, as if thumbing his nose, "J'suis porteur, moi!" The captain shook his fist and raced down the ladder and rushed forward to the bow, as angry a ship's officer as Mr. Poulter, who was now too interested to care whether the ship sailed or not, had ever seen. Under the captain's personal direction more bars were fetched. But it was plain that he had offended the workmen's proud spirits, and that now they too didn't much care whether the ship sailed or not. They pushed back their caps, lit cigarettes, and tried a little concerted mesmerism on the cable. This did no good. The captain flung down his megaphone, dashed up the ladder to the bridge, and disappeared into the wheelhouse. After a moment — during which he must have jerked the engine-room telegraphs to full speed astern — he came out again on the starboard wing to watch results.

The ship quivered, settled, then leaped. The cable took the strain and for an instant held. Then it snapped, near the bollard. The long end coiled swiftly back toward the ship, causing the blond to skip away from the rail right into the arms of the black one with the waxed moustache, who held her tight — *la pauvre petite*. The captain nodded, pleased with his manoeuvre; the ship continued to back, then turned and headed for the Channel.

"The whole affair," concluded Mr. Poulter, "was most disturbing from the point of view of proper seamanship. It couldn't conceivably have happened that way in England. In the first place, the cable wouldn't have jammed. Secondly, if it had jammed, the first officer would have quietly issued the right orders; the proper tools for cutting the cable would have been produced through the proper channels, and cheerily, smartly, the ship would have been freed. It is not unlikely — or no, it is a *possibility* — that an attempt would have been made to saw through the bollard instead of the cable, and that the whole affair might have taken a couple of hours instead of the fifteen minutes it took the French captain to release his ship by the simple use of *Système D*. But you may be sure that there would have been no shouting between bridge and dock, no running about; the captain would most certainly not have appeared in the affair at all. And, I'm afraid, it wouldn't have been any fun at all," Mr. Poulter ended regretfully.

The first thing anyone thinks of when he sees the coast of his homeland shrink away into a little spot, and then nothing, is that special someone he is leaving behind (after looking around at his fellow passengers, one who is accompanied by that special someone might think of the special someone he wishes he were leaving behind). Lord Byron's Don Juan (to keep the meter, pronounce it the English way: Don Jew'-an) was always leaving a woman behind. Here's how he felt the first time he sailed away from one, or two, or . . .

Lord Byron
Love Sick *c1820*

Don Juan bade his valet pack his things
   According to direction, then received
A lecture and some money: for four springs
   He was to travel; and though Inez grieved
(As every kind of parting has its stings),
   She hoped he would improve — perhaps believed.
A letter, too, she gave (he never read it)
Of good advice — and two or three of credit . . .

Juan embarked — the ship got under way,
   The wind was fair, the water passing rough;
A devil of a sea rolls in that bay,
   As I, who've crossed it oft, know well enough;
And, standing upon deck, the dashing spray
   Flies in one's face, and makes it weather-tough;
And there he stood to take, and take again,
His first — perhaps his last — farewell of Spain.

I can't but say it is an awkward sight
   To see one's native land receding through
The growing waters; it unmans one quite,
   Especially when life is rather new.
I recollect Great Britain's coast looks white,

But almost every other country's blue,
When gazing on them, mystified by distance,
We enter on our nautical existence . . .

Don Juan stood, and, gazing from the stern,
    Beheld his native Spain receding far;
First partings form a lesson hard to learn,
    Even nations feel this when they go to war;
There is a sort of unexprest concern,
    A kind of shock that sets one's heart ajar;
At leaving even the most unpleasant people
And places, one keeps looking at the steeple.

But Juan had got many things to leave,
    His mother, and a mistress, and no wife,
So that he had much better cause to grieve
    Than many persons more advanced in life;
And if we now and then a sigh must heave
    At quitting even those we quit in strife,
No doubt we weep for those the heart endears —
That is, till deeper griefs congeal our tears . . .

And Juan wept, and much he sighed and thought,
    While his salt tears dropped into the salt sea,
"Sweets to the sweet" (I have so much to quote;
You must excuse this extract — 'tis where she,
The Queen of Denmark, for Ophelia brought
    Flowers to the grave); and, sobbing often, he
Reflected on his present situation,
And seriously resolved on reformation.

"Farewell, my Spain — a long farewell!" he cried.
    "Perhaps I may revisit thee no more,
But die, as many an exiled heart hath died,
    Of its own thirst to see again thy shore.
Farewell, where Guadalquivir's waters glide!
    Farewell, my mother! And, since all is o'er,
Farewell, too, dearest Julia!" (Here he drew
Her letter out again, and read it through.)

"And oh! if e'er I should forget, I swear —
    But that's impossible, and cannot be —
Sooner shall this blue ocean melt to air,
    Sooner shall earth resolve itself to sea,
Than I resign thine image, oh, my fair!

Or think of anything excepting thee;
A mind diseased no remedy can physic."
(Here the ship gave a lurch and he grew sea-sick.)
"Sooner shall heaven kiss earth!" (Here he fell sicker.)
     "Oh, Julia! what is every other woe?
(For God's sake let me have a glass of liquor;
     Pedro, Battista, help me down below.)
Julia, my love! (you rascal, Pedro, quicker)
     Oh, Julia! (this curst vessel pitches so)
Beloved Julia, hear me still beseeching!"
(Here he grew inarticulate with retching.)

He felt that chilling heaviness of heart,
     Or rather stomach, which, alas! attends,
Beyond the best apothecary's art,
     The loss of love, the treachery of friends,
Or death of those we dote on, when a part
     Of us dies with them as each fond hope ends.
No doubt he would have been much more pathetic,
But the sea acted as a strong emetic.

Love's a capricious power: I've known it hold
     Out through a fever caused by its own heat,
But be much puzzled by a cough and cold,
     And find a quinsy very hard to treat;
Against all noble maladies he's bold
     But vulgar illnesses don't like to meet,
Nor that a sneeze should interrupt his sigh,
Nor inflammations redden his blind eye.

But worst of all is nausea, or a pain
     About the lower region of the bowels;
Love, who heroically breathes a vein,
     Shrinks from the application of hot towels,
And purgatives are dangerous to his reign,
     Sea-sickness death. His love was perfect, how else
Could Juan's passion, while the billows roar,
Resist his stomach, ne'er at sea before?

Name That Tune

*T*he next morning we weighed anchor and went to sea. It was a great happiness to get away, after this dragging, dispiriting delay. I thought there never was such gladness in the air before, such brightness in the sun, such beauty in the sea. I was satisfied with the picnic, then, and with all its belongings. All my malicious instincts were dead within me; and as America faded out of sight, I think a spirit of charity rose up in their place that was as boundless, for the time being, as the broad ocean that was heaving its billows about us. I wished to express my feelings — I wished to lift up my voice and sing; but I did not know anything to sing, and so I was obliged to give up the idea. It was no loss to the ship though, perhaps. — *Mark Twain, 1869.*

"To tell you the truth, Chief, I'd almost given up hope of an ill wind this trip."

❧Seasickness

❧*Fortunately, most cruise ships don't heave and ho like they used to in Byron's day, or even in our parents'. However, we can't let technology stand in the way of all the humor that took as its target the least funny thing that normally occurs on board. Seasickness is to the ocean cruise as the stumble is to walking: it brings us all down together, or nearly all of us (the others give us someone to despise).*

Humorists have even found good things to say about the Dread Disease. Petroleum V. Nasby, one of America's greatest political humorists, wrote, "There is one good thing about sea-sickness, and only one: the sufferer cannot possibly have any other disease at the same time." Harriet Beecher Stowe, best known for Uncle Tom's Cabin, *but also a good-humored travel writer in her spare time, found joy in the Great Bane: 'It is really amusing to watch the gradual progress of this epidemic. . . . Your poet launches forth, 'full of sentiment sublime as billows,' discoursing magnificently on the color of the waves and the glory of the clouds; but gradually he grows white about the mouth, gives sidelong looks towards the stairway; at last, with one desperate plunge, he sets, to rise no more."*

Humorists the like of Bill Nye, Benjamin Franklin, Lucy Seaman Bainbridge, George Peck, and Arthur Guiterman saw the comic possibilities inherent in seasickness and rose to the occasion (after lying down for some time, of course).

Bill Nye
A Fair Trade 1881

I HAVE not enjoyed the Exposition so much as I thought I was going to; partly because it has been so infernally hot, and partly because I have been a little homesick. I was very homesick on board ship; very homesick indeed. About all the amusement that we had cross-

ing the wide waste of waters was to go and lean over the ship's railing
by the hour, and telescope the duodenum into the æsophagus. I used
to stand that way and look down into the dark green depths of old
ocean, and wonder what mysterious secrets were hidden beneath the
green cold waves and the wide rushing waste of swirling, foamy
waters. I learned to love this weird picture at last, and used to go out
on deck every morning and swap my breakfast to this priceless pano-
rama for the privilege of watching it all day.

Benjamin Franklin
Claims of the Sea 1767

AT Dover, the next morning, we embarked for Calais with a number of passengers, who had never before been at sea. They
would previously make a hearty breakfast, because if the wind
should fail, we might not get over till supper time. Doubtless they
thought, that when they had paid for their breakfast they had a right
to it, and that when they had swallowed it they were sure of it. But
they had scarce been out half an hour, before the sea laid claim to it,
and they were obliged to deliver it up. So that it seems there are
uncertainties, even beyond those between the cup and the lip. If ever
you go to sea, take my advice and live sparingly a day or two beforehand. The sickness, if any, will be lighter and sooner over.

Lucy Seaman Bainbridge
Pet Theories 1882

EVERYBODY has a pet theory about seasickness, and the less one
knows experimentally of winds and waves, the stronger is he in
the opinion that he has discovered a sure remedy or unfailing preventive for such attacks. Before starting on this first voyage of the world
tour, my friends all along the way had confidentially imparted to me
their secret. Said one, "The difficulty is not in the stomach, it's in the
head; and you must take hyoscyamus and nux vomica." So I bought a
bottle of each. Another said in a tone of great wisdom, "The seat of
the disturbance in so-called sea-sickness is at the base of the brain.
The remedy is simple, but sure; you must apply brown paper wet in
vinegar." So I bought brown paper and trusted to the ship steward for
vinegar. "Nothing like lemons," said an old friend. So we laid in a
stock of lemons. "But," said a gentleman to me, "I know positively

what will prevent mal de mer, if you are willing to try it. Keep drinking raw whiskey when first you embark, until — well, until you are
drunk; and when you come out of it you will be all right for the rest
of the trip." I thought that prescription over carefully, and concluded
that the remedy was worse than the disease. I did not lay in a supply
of whiskey. Said a lady who had never been to sea, but her second
cousin had, "I am going to tell you of a new and perfect preventive; it
cannot fail. Take strips of cloth a few inches wide and sew them
together; then bind the body very tightly." A dry goods dealer in San
Francisco sold me several yards of cotton cloth. It was torn in strips
exactly according to directions, and for awhile I became more like an
Egyptian mummy than a living American. Said one, "Don't eat a
mouthful for twenty-four hours before stepping on board your
steamer!" But said another. "Be sure and eat a good square meal the
very last thing before you leave land." Not being able to carry out
both directions, I chose the latter. I will not enumerate the score of
other specifics: suffice it to say I tried them nearly all, singly and col-
lectively, and my experience with them could be expressed in the
words of Solomon: "All is vanity and vexation of spirit." For days I
could claim kinship with the man who went to sea and at first felt so
badly he was afraid he would die, and next afraid he wouldn't.

George Peck
The Sea-Sick Princess 1884

A DISPATCH from Boston says that the Princess Louise was greatly
weakened by the strain she was compelled to undergo during
the tempestuous voyage from Bermuda to Providence. She was sea-
sick all the time, and could not rest a minute. It is sad to think that
title and wealth does not exempt the possessor from the annoyances
that ordinary poor, untitled persons have, when traveling. What
does the fact of being the daughter of a queen amount to, if one must
hold the top of her head on and lean over the railing of a boat, and
"yee-haw" the same as a servant girl, and be deathly sick and feel as
though the ocean is coming up and the princess going down, and *vice
versa*. It seems as though there ought to be something invented that
could cure sea-sickness in the royal families, and the world's great
ones; but probably nothing but taking the stomach out and sending
it by express will ever prevent sea-sickness. In sea-sickness, the persons of royal blood realize how little they amount to, and for this
reason sea-sickness is a good thing. The king, or the queen, or the

princess, who can hire or command somebody to do anything for him or her that is unpleasant, finds when it comes to sea-sickness that they have to take their medicine, and do their own grunting, and their own swearing or praying, as the case may be. When the princess started from Bermuda, and the Bermuda onions, that she had eaten, began to assert their independence and show symptoms of a desire to throw off the yoke of oppression and emerge from their bondage, no doubt she felt as though it was the work of an incendiary, or that she had discovered a new dynamite plot, and she would have been glad to have delegated her responsibility in the matter to other hands, or stomachs, but the law of nature is the same with princesses as it is with peasants, and though she sucked a lemon with all her royal vigor, it was no go, and the onions obtained their freedom. On land she was the daughter of a queen, and all heads bowed at her bidding; but as she sat there on a camp stool, with a shawl over her head, her stomach against the railing, and her hands clasping the head that throbbed as though it would split, she had to attend to her own knitting, even as the whale did when Jonah was a cabin passenger in one of the first sea voyages.

Poor girl! How she wished she was home, or dead, or anything for a change. How she wondered, as she loosened her corsets and grasped the rail with both hands, with a convulsive clutch as some former banquet seemed to desire to say a few words on this momentous occasion, how one little number four stomach could contain so much that was of no use on earth. As she gazed into the green water and thought that if she owned it she would plane it down until it was as smooth as a floor, she pictured to herself the Marquis of Lorne, playing fifteen ball pool in Boston, and drinking Canada malt whisky, while she was suffering, and she decided to give him a piece of her mind if she had any peace of mind left, when she met him, for not being present to hold her head, or have a sea-sick duet with her, and then she would have another spasm and want to see her mother. There was one consolation, and one only, to the princess. The servants were all as sick as she was, except one, and the princess would gladly have exchanged places with the Canadian of obscure birth, who sat placidly crocheting a blue dog, and gazing out upon the beautiful sea in a storm, with no sea-sickness. How the princess envied that girl who was not sick. Her father was a fisherman, and the girl had been out in many a storm, and her stomach had got so it would stay right side up in any weather, and near her was a daughter of Queen Victoria, who couldn't tell one minute whether she would have her shoes left on her the next. It is sad enough to be a princess under ordinary circumstances, but to be a sea-sick princess, for four long days and nights, is enough to make one sorry. A fortune awaits the man who will invent something by which a person can hire somebody to be sea-sick.

Arthur Guiterman
Sea-Chill 1933

WHEN Mrs. John Masefield and her husband, the author of "I Must Go Down to the Seas Again," arrived here on a liner, she said to a reporter, "It was too uppy-downy, and Mr. Masefield was ill." — *News Item.*

I must go down to the seas again, where the billows romp
    and reel,
So all I ask is a large ship that rides on an even keel,
And a mild breeze and a broad deck with a slight list to
    leeward,
And a clean chair in a snug nook and a nice, kind steward.

I must go down to the seas again, the sport of wind
    and tide,
As the gray wave and the green wave play leapfrog
    over the side.
And all I want is a glassy calm with bone-dry scupper,
A good book and a warm rug and a light, plain supper.

I must go down to the seas again, though there I'm
    a total loss,
And can't say which is worst, the pitch, the plunge, the
    roll, the toss.
But all I ask is a safe retreat in a bar well tended,
And a soft berth and a smooth course till the long
    trip's ended.

No one will ever accuse Mark Twain of consistency. He could see so many comic sides to any situation that he would have been a fool to have aimed for such a serious goal. Here are two short descriptions of a perfectly well Mark Twain on a ship full of perfectly seasick passen-

gers. The first is from Innocents Abroad, *the second from his note-books. The voyage is the same, but not the punchlines.*

Mark Twain
The Joys of Seeing,
the Agony of Having to Hear 1869

BY some happy fortune I was not seasick.—That was a thing to be proud of. I had not always escaped before. If there is one thing in the world that will make a man peculiarly and insufferably self-conceited, it is to have his stomach behave itself, the first day at sea, when nearly all his comrades are seasick. Soon, a venerable fossil, shawled to the chin and bandaged like a mummy, appeared at the door of the after deck-house, and the next lurch of the ship shot him into my arms. I said:

"Good-morning, Sir. It is a fine day."

He put his hand on his stomach and said, "*Oh,* my!" and then staggered away and fell over the coop of a skylight.

Presently another old gentleman was projected from the same door, with great violence. I said:

"Calm yourself, Sir — There is no hurry. It is a fine day, Sir."

He, also, put his hand on his stomach and said, "*Oh,* my!" and reeled away.

In a little while another veteran was discharged abruptly from the same door, clawing at the air for a saving support. I said:

"Good-morning, Sir. It is a fine day for pleasuring. You were about to say —"

"*Oh,* my!"

I thought so. I anticipated *him,* any how. I staid there and was bombarded with old gentlemen for an hour perhaps; and all I got out of them was "*Oh,* my!"

I went away, then, in a thoughtful mood. I said, this is a good pleasure excursion. I like it. The passengers are not garrulous, but still they are sociable. I like those old people, but somehow they all seem to have the "Oh, my" rather bad.

I knew what was the matter with them. They were seasick. And I was glad of it. We all like to see people seasick when we are not, ourselves. Playing whist by the cabin lamps when it is storming outside, is pleasant; walking the quarter-deck in the moonlight, is pleasant; smoking in the breezy foretop is pleasant, when one is not afraid to go up there; but these are all feeble and commonplace compared with the joy of seeing people suffering the miseries of seasickness.

First night a tempest — the greatest seen on this coast for many years — though occupying an outside berth on upper deck it yet did not seem so rough to us as it did to those below and we remained in bed all night, while the other passengers realizing the great danger all got up and dressed.

The ship was down too much by the head, and just doggedly fought the seas, instead of climbing over them.

Nearly everybody seasick. Happily I escaped — Had something worse — lay in bed and received passengers' reports.

ᵃ▶On Board

ᵃ▶*Okay, now we've got that out of our system, we can look at the brighter side of things. Once aboard, the first thing you'll want to do is look around. You'll want to see your cabin and all the elegant facilities. You feel you know them already, having read over and over again those gorgeous brochures that present apparently palatial staterooms from angles it takes a photographer years to learn. You expect the satisfaction of a wonderful déjà vu. Well, Charles Dickens had similar expectations embarking upon his historic trip to the New World.*

Charles Dickens
Going Away 1842

I SHALL never forget the one-fourth serious and three-fourths comical astonishment, with which, on the morning of the third of January, eighteen hundred and forty-two, I opened the door of, and put my head into, a "state-room'" on board the Britannia steam-packet, twelve hundred tons burthen per register, bound for Halifax and Boston, and carrying Her Majesty's mails.

That this state-room had been specially engaged for "Charles Dickens, Esquire, and Lady," was rendered sufficiently clear even to my scared intellect by a very small manuscript, announcing the fact, which was pinned on a very flat quilt, covering a very thin mattress, spread like a surgical plaster on a most inaccessible shelf. But that this was the state-room concerning which Charles Dickens, Esquire, and Lady, had held daily and nightly conferences for at least four months preceding; that this could by any possibility be that small snug chamber of the imagination, which Charles Dickens, Esquire, with the spirit of prophecy strong upon him, had always foretold would contain at least one little sofa, and which his lady, with a modest yet most magnificent sense of its limited dimensions, had

from the first opined would not hold more than two enormous portmanteaus in some odd corner out of sight (portmanteaus which
could now no more be got in at the door, not to say stowed away,
than a giraffe could be persuaded or forced into a flower-pot); that
this utterly impracticable, thoroughly hopeless, and profoundly preposterous box, had the remotest reference to, or connection with,
those chaste and pretty, not to say gorgeous little bowers, sketched
by a masterly hand, in the highly varnished lithographic plan hanging up in the agent's counting-house in the city of London; that this
room of state, in short, could be anything but a pleasant fiction and
cheerful jest of the captain's, invented and put in practice for the better relish and enjoyment of the real state-room presently to be dis-
closed: — these were truths which I really could not, for the
moment, bring my mind at all to bear upon or comprehend. And I
sat down upon a kind of horsehair slab, or perch, of which there
were two within; and looked, without any expression of countenance whatever, at some friends who had come on board with us,
and who were crushing their faces into all manner of shapes by
endeavouring to squeeze them through the small doorway.

We had experienced a pretty smart shock before coming below,
which, but that we were the most sanguine people living, might have
prepared us for the worst. The imaginative artist to whom I have
already made allusion, has depicted in the same great work a chamber of almost interminable perspective, furnished, as Mr. Robins
would say, in a style of more than eastern splendour, and filled (but
not inconveniently so) with groups of ladies and gentlemen, in the
very highest state of enjoyment and vivacity. Before descending into
the bowels of the ship, we had passed from the deck into a long narrow apartment, not unlike a gigantic hearse with windows in the
sides; having at the upper end a melancholy stove, at which three or
four chilly stewards were warming their hands, while on either side,
extending down its whole dreary length, was a long, long table, over
each of which a rack, fixed to the low roof, and stuck full of drinking
glasses and cruet-stands, hinted dismally at rolling seas, and heavy
weather. I had not at that time seen the ideal presentment of this
chamber which has since gratified me so much, but I observed that
one of our friends, who had made the arrangements for our voyage,
turned pale on entering, retreated on the friend behind him, smote
his forehead involuntarily, and said below his breath, "Impossible! it
cannot be!" or words to that effect. He recovered himself however by
a great effort, and, after a preparatory cough or two, cried, with a
ghastly smile which is still before me, looking at the same time round

the walls, "Ha! the breakfast-room, steward — eh?" We all foresaw what the answer must be: we knew the agony he suffered. He had often spoken of *the saloon;* had taken in and lived upon the pictorial idea; had usually given us to understand, at home, that to form a just conception of it it would be necessary to multiply the size and furniture of an ordinary drawing-room by seven, and then fall short of the reality. When the man in reply avowed the truth — the blunt, remorseless, naked truth — "This is the saloon, sir" — he actually reeled beneath the blow.

In persons who were so soon to part, and interpose between their else daily communication the formidable barrier of many thousand miles of stormy space, and who were for that reason anxious to cast no other cloud, not even the passing shadow of a moment's disappointment or discomfiture, upon the short interval of happy companionship that yet remained to them — in persons so situated, the natural transition from these first surprises was obviously into peals of hearty laughter; and I can report that I, for one, being still seated upon the slab or perch before mentioned, roared outright until the vessel rang again. Thus, in less than two minutes after coming upon it for the first time, we all by common consent agreed that this stateroom was the pleasantest and most facetious and capital contrivance possible; and that to have had it one inch larger would have been quite a disagreeable and deplorable state of things. And with this, and with showing how, — by very nearly closing the door, and twining in and out like serpents, and by counting the little washing slab as standing-room, — we could manage to insinuate four people into it, all at one time; and entreating each other to observe how very airy it was (in dock), and how there was a beautiful port-hole which could be kept open all day (weather permitting), and how there was quite a large bull's eye just over the looking-glass which would render shaving a perfectly easy and delightful process (when the ship didn't roll too much), we arrived, at last, at the unanimous conclusion that it was rather spacious than otherwise; though I do verily believe that, deducting the two berths, one above the other, than which nothing smaller for sleeping in was ever made except coffins, it was no bigger than one of those hackney cabriolets which have the door behind, and shoot their fares out, like sacks of coals, upon the pavement.

Ah, life on board, decked out in as little as we choose, so many alternatives and no requirements, fresh air, fresh fish, fresh propositions. Let's start with the first night out, with how Christopher Morley's protagonist in The Arrow *learned to love the sea and how Harriet Beecher Stowe was nearly overcome by nightfears of the deep.*

Christopher Morley
A Pounding Hum c1930

I SUPPOSE the reason why cabin stewards fold them like that, instead of tucking 'em in as bedclothes are arranged on shore, is that if the ship founders you can get out of your bunk so much quicker. The life preservers are up there, on top of the little wardrobe. The picture of Mr. Boddy-Finch, the resolute-looking man with a moustache, showing how to wear the life waistcoat, is on the panel by the door. Mr. Boddy-Finch's moustache has a glossy twist, probably waxed like that to keep it from getting wet while he's demonstrating his waistcoat. He guarantees that the thing will keep you afloat for forty-eight hours: how can he tell unless he's tried it? Amusing scene, Mr. Boddy-Finch floating competently in the Mersey while a jury of shipowners on the dock cheer him on toward the forty-eighth hour.

So he was thinking as he got into the berth and carefully snugged himself into the clothes that were folded, not tucked. The detective story slid down beside the pillow. No bed companion is so soothing as a book you don't intend to read. He had realized just now that the strangeness had worn off. This was his first voyage. He had supposed, of course, he would be ill, but he had never felt more at home, physically, in his life. The distemper that had burdened him was of another sort; but now it was gone — gone so quietly and completely that he hardly missed it yet. He only knew that some secretive instinct had brought him early to his bunk, not to sleep, but because there, in that narrow solitude, he could examine the queer delicious mood now pervading him.

The steady drum and quiver of a slow ship finding her own comfortable way through heavy sea. The little stateroom, which he had to himself, was well down and amidships; the great double crash and rhythm of the engines was already part of his life. A pounding hum, pounding hum, pounding hum. He invented imitative phrases to accompany that cadence. Oh, lyric love, half piston and half crank! Roofed over by the upper berth, shaded from the lamp by the clicking chintz curtain, this was his lair to spy out on the laws of life. He could see his small snug dwelling sink and sway. Marvellous cradling ease, sweet equation of all forces. He studied the pattern of honest bolts in the white iron ceiling. Surely, with reference to himself, they were rigid: yet he saw them rise and dip and swing. The corridor outside was one long creak. There was a dropping sag of his berth as it caved beneath him, then a climbing push as it rose, pressing under his shoulders. He waited, in curious lightness and thrill, to feel the long slow lift, the hanging pause, the beautiful sinking plunge. The downward slope then gently tilted sideways. His knees pressed hard against the board, he could see his toothbrush glide across the tumbler. He was incredibly happy in an easy bliss. This primitive cycle of movement seemed a part of the secret rhymes of biology. Now he understood why sailors often feel ill when they reach the dull, flat solidity of earth.

The lull and ecstasy of the sea is what man was meant for. The whole swinging universe takes you up in its arms, and you know both desire and fulfilment. And down below, from far within, like — oh, like things you believed you'd forgotten — that steady, grumbling hum. The first night he was a bit anxious when she rolled: his entrails yawned when she leaned over so heavily on emptiness. But then he had divined something; it is the things that frighten you that are really worth while. Now, when she canted, he did not hold back; he leaned with her, as though eager to come as close as possible to that seethe and hiss along her dripping side. It was the inexpressive faces of stewards and stewardesses that had best fortified him. They stood on duty along the exclaiming passages, priests of this white ritual world. Their sallow sexton faces seemed gravely reassuring the congregation that all was calculated, charted, and planned. They flexed and balanced serenely like vicars turning eastward at the appointed clause. He had barely escaped horrifying one of them, his bedroom steward who came in suddenly — the door was open — while he was doing a private caper of triumph at realizing he wasn't ill. He repeated his silly chant, smiling in the berth:

> "Wallow in a hollow with a pounding hum,
> Pillow on a billow with a pounding hum,
> Now the Atlantic
> Drives me frantic,
> Pounding pounding pounding hum!"

Harriet Beecher Stowe
Night on Shipboard 1854

AT night! — the beauties of a night on shipboard! — down in your berth, with the sea hissing and fizzing, gurgling and booming, within an inch of your ear; and then the steward comes along at twelve o'clock and puts out your light, and there you are! Jonah in the whale was not darker or more dismal. There, in profound ignorance and blindness, you lie, and feel yourself rolled upwards, and downwards, and sidewise, and all ways, like a cork in a tub of water; much such a sensation as one might suppose it to be, were one headed up in a barrel and thrown into the sea.

Occasionally a wave comes with a thump against your ear, as if a great hammer were knocking on your barrel, to see that all within was safe and sound. Then you begin to think of krakens, and sharks, and porpoises, and sea serpents, and all the monstrous, slimy, cold, hobgoblin brood, who, perhaps, are your next door neighbors; and the old blue-haired Ocean whispers through the planks, "Here you are; I've got you. Your grand ship is my plaything. I can do what I like with it."

Then you hear every kind of odd noise in the ship — creaking, straining, crunching, scraping, pounding, whistling, blowing off steam, each of which to your unpractised ear is significant of some impending catastrophe; you lie wide awake, listening with all your might, as if your watching did any good, till at last sleep overcomes you, and the morning light convinces you that nothing very particular has been the matter, and that all these frightful noises are only the necessary attendants of what is called a good run.

It is said that a great mind can synthesize, and occasionally anaesthesize, massive amounts of experience into a single image. H. L. Mencken had so great a mind, he managed twenty-two. Other great minds tend effusively toward the romantic, for example, the passenger in the following poem by Oliver Wendell Holmes, Sr., the judge's medical father and a famous New England wit. Fortunately, the first requirement of humor accompanied Holmes's passenger: another person, and one as unlike him as possible.

H. L. Mencken
The High Seas 1924

THE kid who sits in the bucket of tar. . . . The buxom stewardess who comes in and inquires archly if one rang . . . The humorous piano-tuner who tunes the grand piano in the music-room in the 15-16ths-tone scale. . . . The electric fan which, when a stray zephyr blows in through the porthole, makes a noise like a dentist's drill. . . . The alien ship's printer who, in the daily wireless paper, reports a baseball score of 165 to 3. . . . The free Christian Science literature in the reading-room. . . . The pens in the writing-room. . . . The elderly Grosshändler with the young wife. . . . The red-haired girl in the green sweater. . . . The retired bootlegger disguised as a stock-broker. . . . The stockbroker disguised as a United States Senator. . . . The boy who climbs into the lifeboat. . . . The chief steward wearing the No. 18¾ collar. . . . The mysterious pipes that run along the stateroom ceilings. . . . The discovery that one forgot to pack enough undershirts. . . . The night watchman who raps on the door at 3.30 A.M. to deliver a wireless message reading "Sorry missed you. Bon voyage" . . . The bartender who adds a dash of witchhazel to cocktails. . . . The wilting flowers standing in ice-pitchers and spittoons in the hallways. . . . The fight in the steerage. . . . The old lady who gets stewed and sends for the doctor. . . . The news that the ship is in Long. 43°, 41′, 16″ W, Lat. 40°, 23′, 39″ N. . . . The report that the starboard propeller has lost a blade.

Oliver Wendell Holmes, Sr.
A Sea Dialogue

CABIN PASSENGER

Friend, you seem thoughtful. I not wonder much
That he who sails the ocean should be sad.
I am myself reflective. When I think
Of all this wallowing beast, the Sea, has sucked
Between his sharp thin lips, the wedgy waves,
What heaps of diamonds, rubies, emeralds, pearls;
What piles of shekels, talents, ducats, crowns,
What bales of Tyrian mantles, Indian shawls,
Of laces that have blanked the weavers' eyes,
Of silken tissues, wrought by worm and man,

The half-starved workman, and the well-fed worm;
What marbles, bronzes, pictures, parchments, books;
What many-lobuled, thought-engendering brains;
Lie with the gaping sea-shells in his maw, —
I, too, am silent; for all language seems
A mockery, and the speech of man is vain.
O mariner, we look upon the waves
And they rebuke our babbling. 'Peace!' they say, —
'Mortal, be still!" My noisy tongue is hushed,
And with my trembling finger on my lips
My soul exclaims in ecstasy —

MAN AT WHEEL
Belay!

CABIN PASSENGER
Ah yes! 'Delay,' — it calls, 'nor haste to break
The charm of stillness with an idle word!'
O mariner, I love thee, for thy thought
Strides even with my own, nay, flies before.
Thou art a brother to the wind and wave;
Have they not music for thine ear as mine,
When the wild tempest makes thy ship his lyre,
Smiting a cavernous basso from the shrouds
And climbing up his gamut through the stays,
Through buntlines, bowlines, ratlines, till it shrills
An alto keener than the locust sings,
And all the great Aeolian orchestra
Storms out its mad sonata in the gale?
Is not the scene a wondrous and —

MAN AT WHEEL
Avast!

CABIN PASSENGER
Ah yes, a vast, a vast and wondrous scene!
I see thy soul is open as the day
That holds the sunshine in its azure bowl
To all the solemn glories of the deep.
Tell me, O mariner, dost thou never feel
The grandeur of thine office, — to control
The keel that cuts the ocean like a knife

And leaves a wake behind it like a seam
In the great shining garment of the world?

Belay y'r jaw, y' swab! y' hoss-marine!
(To the Captain.)
Ah, ay, Sir! Stiddy, Sir! Sou'wes'-b'sou'!

ACTIVITIES

☙Eating and Drinking

☙*Once the morning comes (or the rosy-fingered dawn appears, if you're in the Aegean), the first thought is, what will I do with myself? Am I going to get myself into shape or just relax, read and spectate, particularly around the pool? Am I going to give up my diet, give in to the insistent dining opportunities, or will I be loyal and true (to what, to whom?)? How early should I start drinking? — what with no work — and how much? — what with no car to drive home. Bone up on the places I'll visit, play cards, meet people, flirt? Breakfast wins, of course, because, without any mountains around, it's it that's there. On the open sea, food is always there, mountains of it.*

Nicholas Coleridge
High Caloric Orgies 1985

IF a week is a long time in politics, then a week on the Pacific is a lifetime. Especially when you are marooned three thousand miles from anywhere with the Flintstones. Not that my fellow American passengers kept pet dinosaurs, but they shared Fred and Barney's round-the-clock obsession with junk food. Travelling by freighter there is little to do except anticipate the next meal, and these high calorie orgies followed each other with barely an hour's respite in between. Some of the passengers were so obese that they couldn't sit down in the ship's armchairs, only on the sofas; still they thought of nothing beyond their enormous appetites and the means of satiating them. Four times a day they scrutinised the small type of the menu, debating how much food they could reasonably order before the chef closed the kitchen.

"Hey, steward, get me a short beef with spaghetti, and a side order of Mexican enchiladas, burritos and tamales. And a plate of corn fritters with fried rice. And if you've got any of that blueberry pie a la mode fetch me out a slice of that. No, make that two slices — with topping, for sure. And bag me up a turkey club sandwich in foil to carry out."

There seemed a very real danger of our running out of food before reaching the International Dateline and I began to hoard Saltine crackers and cubes of Jell-O in my cabin as hostages to fortune.

Four nights out of the eight-day voyage we put our clocks forward one hour. These twenty-three hour days made the constant eating even more oppressive, since the meals were crammed into truncated timetables. The storm made it impossible to sleep at night, so the passengers dozed by day, rendering it ever more difficult to tell whether it was breakfast, lunch, dinner or supper we were awaiting. Certainly the menu held no clues.

The voyage took on the quality of an existentialist play in which the characters baffle the audience with an obscure parable of life in purgatory, set in the saloon of a steamship. Only the spontaneous orders to the steward proved the performance was unscripted.

"Hey steward, got any more of that coconut cake?"

"Hey steward, how come I don't get any eggs with my hash browns?"

Conversations carried over from one meal to the next, with no acknowledgement of passing time. A question posed on the hundred and fifty degree latitude could be answered fifteen hundred miles further on, on the hundred and sixty-fifth degree. Our observations became diffuse and unrelated.

"Jimmy makes his own barbecue sauce, it's so tasty with corn fritters."

"When we have guests turn up unexpectedly, do you know what I make for them? Trifle! That's right, a trifle. I guess I use up all Erwin's Grand Marnier that way."

"This meat makes me kind of nostalgic for Pebbles."

"Pebbles?"

"Our dawg. His dawg mix reminds me of this oxtail."

"They're featuring pastrami on rye for dinner with potato salad."

"Do you know something, Nicholas, I was disappointed with Japanese food. Somehow, I don't know, I expected it to be more different."

"Pebbles used to like pastrami, remember?"

"Japanese food isn't *different?*" This was Erwin speaking. "Have you tried kochee — you can smell it four blocks away."

"Tell me, Nicholas. Is it true you still have hot water radiators in London?"

"So my best Grand Marnier goes into your goddam trifle, does it?"

It hasn't always been so easy to eat and drink on shipboard. In the old days of mal de mer *and steerage, eating could be an adventure; the following excerpt from the early-nineteenth-century travels of George Pinckard will make you appreciate whatever they put in front of you, simply for the fact that it remains there. As for drinking, there's not much challenge and excitement these days to having a drink or two aboard an ocean liner. There's less roll than there used to be, and the bottles are the same ones you had back on shore, only more plentiful. Things were much more fun in the days of Prohibition, as Frank Ward O'Malley relates with the most Irish of wits.*

George Pinckard
Our Dinner Ceremony 1806

OUR dinner ceremony is often rendered a humorous scene: at this hour the cabin being the general rendezvous of the party, we meet — crawl, trembling, towards the table — and tie ourselves in the chairs. A tray is set before us, with deep holes cut in it for the dishes, plates, and glasses; the table and chairs are lashed to the deck; yet one or other frequently gives way and upsets half the things in the cabin! Presently enters the steward with soup, followed by his little slave with potatoes; and the servants with such other covers as there may chance to be. But scarcely are the things upon table, and the servants stationed, clinging to the backs of our chairs, before a sudden lurch of the ship tumbles all into disorder. Away go steward, servants, and little Mungo, to the lee-corner of the cabin: the soup salutes the lap of one of us; another receives a leg of pork; a third is presented with a piece of mutton or beef; a couple of chickens or ducks fly to another; the pudding jumps nearly into the mouth of the next; and the potatoes are tossed in all directions about the deck of the cabin. One saves his plate; another stops his knife and fork; some cling to the table, thinking only of saving their persons; one secures the bottle; another, half fallen, holds up his glass in one hand and fixes himself fast to his chair with the other. Chaos is renewed! everything is in motion — everything in disorder and confusion. At the next roll of the ship the servants, staring with amazement, again *fetch way,* and, with extended arms, are tossed to the opposite side of the cabin, where they cling fast and remain fixed as statues, afraid again to move: and, although we are lashed in the chairs ourselves, it is with difficulty we can maintain our seats. Plates, dishes, knives, forks, and glasses clatter together in all the discord of the moment:

the steward and his boy, crawling upon their hands and knees after the dancing potatoes, the flying fowls, or walking joints, are rolled over and over at our feet; and all is disorder and confusion. The ship now becomes steady for a moment; the scattered parts of the dinner are collected; and those who have escaped sickness again attempt to eat. Some, forseeing all these accidents, fix themselves in a corner upon the cabin-deck, and take the plate between their knees, fancying themselves in security: but, quickly, they are tumbled, in ridiculous postures, to the other side of the cabin, sprawling, with outstretched limbs, like frightened crabs. Some, having no calls of appetite, join not in the feast, but lie swinging up and down in their cots or hammocks; others remain rolling from side to side in their berths. Some cry out with sore bruises; some from being wetted with the sprays: one calls for help; another relieves his stomach from sickness; while others, lamenting only their dinner, loudly bewail the soup, the meat, and the pudding. Some abuse the helmsman; others the ship; and others the sea; while all join in a chorus of imprecations upon the wind.

Frank Ward O'Malley
Shipping the Claret to Port 1922

A SHIP'S bellhop came along the decks distributing dainty little booklets.

"The passenger list," said someone, reaching for one of the booklets.

I opened my copy without glancing at preambles and began on the A page the always interesting study of the names of one's fellow passengers.

Aldegunder, Palmberg. Alfer, Herrenberg.
Alsheimer, Sonnenberg.

"All particularly masterful master bakers," I mused, "who no doubt can afford to travel first-class."

Lightly my eye glanced at a name here, another there:

Berncastler, Reisling.
Deidescheimer, Nueberg.
Duerkheimer, Reisling.
Haig & Haig.
Hennessey, John.

I flipped the pages feverishly:

Jameson, John.
MacDonald, Sandy.
Walker, Johnny.

It was unbelievable! Could it be possible that so many celebrities — at least one man of international fame topping any letter grouping one turned to — were aboard one ship? Perhaps just one of the Haig boys might be with us, yes; but certainly common business sense, especially common Scotch business sense, would cause the Haig family to see to it that one of the boys stayed safely ashore while the other was risking the dangers of the sea.

I turned back to the booklet cover for enlightenment. The big block printing on the cover explained all:

WINE LIST

ALSO

SPIRITS, LIQUEURS, COCKTAILS

AND

BEERS

"Queer people, you Americans." Thus I began tentative acquaint-anceship with the man, also reading the wine list, in the deck chair at my right. He was a prominent New York business man named Mr. I. A. Kettz — Ignatius Aloysius Kettz, I think, although my mere guess about his given names may be all wrong.

"Have we reached the three-mile limit yet?" was Mr. Kettz's only comment.

"No, not yet," drawled a lanky New Englander sprawling all over the deck chair to my left. The lanky New Englander was, if memory does not trick me, a Mr. Abromawitz, of Boston, and he was in men's underwear — his business, I mean.

"Gentlemen," boomed a big voice from the chair to the left of Mr. Abromawitz's, "if I may introduce myself, my name is Finnigan — Michael Finnigan."

I did not know at the instant that Michael Finnigan and I were to be inseparables throughout the rest of the trip. All I was conscious of was that the mere name, Michael Finnigan, aroused in me an over-whelming atavic complex of remote caveman origin. I jumped to my feet with the hot purpose of dragging Michael Finnigan down to my chair and smothering him with one long passionate kiss. But his bris-tling red beard calmed me. Gripping myself I shook his hand.

"It's impossible, gentlemen," began the lanky New Englander, Mr. Abromawitz, "to run a transatlantic passenger service without a smoking-room bar. As a business man I ask you how——"

That was as far as he got. Wild-eyed men suddenly began to run past us, crying out excitedly. Women were crying out in terror and pointing hysterically toward the opposite, or port side of the ship.

It seems that one of the breed that is always ready to yell "Fire!" on the slightest pretext in a crowded theater was aboard. The idiot — he was a rangy Middle Westerner named Splitzenheim, from Pittsburgh, I believe — had not yelled "Fire!" He had done worse. He had spread the ghoulish story that the skipper had, half mile or so on the bad, or land side of the three-mile limit, pointed the ship more and more to the northeast until now the liner, still inside the three-mile limit, was running parallel with the Long Island coast.

Rumors piled high. The skipper was born and raised in Maine, someone recalled. What was Maine? A rock-and-rye ribbed coast girding the first state in the Union to go dry, the American birthplace of prohibition. This captain was one of them!

All passengers now were jammed on the port decks, gazing toward the too close coast of Long Island. Indeed, to all appearances the ship and Long Island appeared to be racing along together, with the bow of Long Island so far ahead of the ship's bow that a day might elapse before we could get a three-mile lead on Long Island.

Mutinous talk began to rumble.

"Gentlemen!" at last shouted a tall Southerner whose broad shoulders loomed large above the angry crowd jamming the port deck — the indignant Southerner was, as I recall the name, a Mr. Geltsticker, of Gumbo, Louisiana — "I propose, gentlemen," continued the dashing Southern colonel, "that a committee of protest right away go quick up to the captain and — and ——"

Speechless, the distinguished-looking Southerner faltered, stopped. Just what it was that the hot-blooded Southerner's committee was to tell the captain never was learned. Rigidly he stood at gaze, high on the deck chair on which he had climbed, his eyes looking steadily through a porthole just opposite where he stood. And next, with a maniacal cry, half sob and half terrible laughter, he flung himself down on the astounded mob and fought and clawed his way toward a smoking-room entrance close to the porthole through which he had been looking.

At the height of his exordium from the deck chair, it seems, Mr. Geltsticker had seen the entire roster of the starboard and port bartenders' first dogwatch file into the smoking room, unlock the bar and pipe all hands to grog.

Little remains to be told.

Let me merely add that never shall I forget that first rush. Among all its wild scenes always, too, I shall remember how a wide, rawboned Texan of obvious frontiersman type — we learned later he was a Mr. S. Pincus, of Curley Wolf, Texas — became wedged at the hip pockets in the smoking-room entrance, blocking all traffic. Kicking him from behind only wedged him the tighter. Strong men behind him screamed and wept in their desperation.

"Around to the other porch of the ship, men!" rang the gallant cry of a New Yorker. I forget his name — it doesn't matter.

Round the ship they raced, galloping forward the length of the port deck and then doubling back on the opposite deck to a starboard entrance to the smoking room, far aft. Their parched tongues hung out as they raced. It was pitiful.

Just to keep the record straight I should like to be able to give here the name of the winner of that round-the-ship sprint, but the name escapes me. I think he was a college athlete; at any rate he was a student from New York City.

It was three o'clock in the afternoon precisely when the hot-blooded Southern orator, Mr. Geltsticker — why is it these old Southern boys of the blood are all born orators? — saw the bar opened. By 3:02 o'clock the smoking-room cash registers were ringing with the uninterrupted steadiness of a railroad crossing's warning bell. Another two minutes later the smoking room was as solidly stuffed as a Philadelphia ballot box always was stuffed on the Sunday night before the Tuesday after the first Monday in November, back in the old days.

In those first moments of German frightfulness one with a name like mine of course stood no chance. How Michael Finnigan secured a good place, his right resting on the bar itself, I could not understand; at least not then.

I could see him inside a few feet from where I stood outside.

The best I got was a place at a smoking-room porthole, but outside looking in. I was one of a long waiting list. We could stand and wait, but were not served. As hour after hour after hour passed, the sun blistering our necks on deck, the slosh and splash of the ice-cold real thing in Pilsener coming to us through the open portholes from within, we who panted for admission to the exclusive club inside prayed that a club member would drop dead, and thus create a vacancy.

Late in the afternoon we had new cause for hope. A grizzled sailorman lugging a stout piece of canvas — the canvas was just about large enough to wrap round a bloated human body, we noted — came to a halt outside the entrance to the smoking room and spread the canvas on deck. Hope jumped to the zenith when the sailorman next brought forth stout sail needles and coarse threads.

We cheered when finally the old salt stepped aft a bit and promptly returned with weighty lumps of scrap iron, of the sort used to sink a body buried at sea.

Goody, goody! Somebody indoors who couldn't handle the stuff had died!

For two hours and forty minutes by our watches the sailorman stitched and stitched. As dusk was settling on the sea he had sewed the canvas to a shape roughly the length and possibly the breadth of a man who had died from guzzling Pilsener from three o'clock in the afternoon until late summer sunset.

The sailor's hard afternoon of work completed, he dragged canvas and weights toward what remained of the barrels of beer on deck and tried to fit the canvas jacket over the cakes of ice piled on top of the beer barrels. The canvas covering for the ice was too small. Chagrined, the sailorman wrapped the scrap iron in the canvas, chucked the afternoon's work overboard and proceeded aft to take up his next important duty.

One man did drop in his tracks just as darkness set in. Unfortunately he was merely another of the overflow standing outside looking in. And oddly enough the venerable gentleman who dropped dead — he was a member of an old New Orleans creole family named Schlippenpfatz, we learned — was the ship's total abstainer.

In justice to the poor old man it should be explained that his doctor was sending him to a German spa to take the cure, because of an illness that had absolutely forced him to go on the wagon. But in spite of great age and illness, he had given the blistering afternoon and evening to climbing furtively, secretly, from the depths of the E deck to the hurricane deck, from stem to stern, on some sort of fruitless search.

I asked him, a moment before he expired in my arms, what he had been seeking. With the last energy left in him he turned his head from side to side, peering about cautiously before answering.

"Dammit all," were his last words, "I was trying to find on this ship a good, reliable, sea-going German bootlegger who would take a chance and slip me a glass of plain water."

At midnight that night, with a nautical "Heave!" and a "Ho!" and a farewell "Atta-boy!" we flipped the old boy over the side.

But enough of the tragedies of the sea.

Some time after the midnight funeral good old Finnigan saved my life. I had felt since the bar opened that if help were to come to me the good Finnigan — who, with the sole exception of myself, was the only passenger aboard with a name like that — alone would help me. Kind flocks to kind.

Following the midnight funeral I had resumed my vigil outside the porthole nearest the smoking-room bar, waiting for someone inside to resign or die, when Finnigan turned and saw me gazing in wistfully only a few feet from where he stood. And immediately Finnigan began to push his way along the bar toward my porthole, cautiously, and always careful not to lose his front-row status. Once during his cautious progress he came close to serious mishap. Someone pushed him so roughly that he all but lost his grip on the edge of the bar — and he told me later he couldn't swim a stroke. Finnigan halted only when he had reached the extreme end of the bar nearest my porthole. He had an idea, and it was wonderful.

"Listen!" he called guardedly across the short space — short but, oh, how long! — separating us. "Borrow the captain's cap and then come back here and I'll tell you how to work it."

The captain, I learned after racing to the bridge, had turned in for the night hours before. The only bluejacket in sight absolutely refused to leave the wheel and rout the captain out of bed. The best that the blue-clad boy at the steering wheel could do for me was to lend me his own sailor cap.

Placing the cap on my head in a jaunty way that made one think of the Prince of Wales, I hurried back though the darkness to my smoking-room porthole. Immediately good old Finnigan directed me to climb up on something, stick my head inside the porthole as far as possible and receive final instructions.

I received them and then proceeded to let loose Finnigan's magnificent idea. For a man with a name like Finnigan he had a sane head.

"Mates!" I yelled to the startled drinking club indoors, my head pressed into the porthole farther, much farther than I could possibly have pressed it on any morning after thereafter. "Mates, attention! I desire officially to announce that the same draft beer you've been drinking here all day and night is being sold at five cents the seidel less in the second-class smoking room. And at even a greater proportionate reduction, mates, the second-class smoking-room bargains on our fine stocks of Kentucky ryes and bourbons, Haig and Haig ——"

I myself couldn't hear the rest of my announcement. Probably in the instant panicky rush toward first-class smoking-room exits no one indoors heard even as far as the name of the second of the Haig boys. There is nothing so excitedly irresistible as a bargain sale to us thrifty old Yanks.

Before the rest of the patient waiting list out in the dark could think, I was inside the now all but vacant smoking room and anchored beside good old Mike Finnigan at the bar. Thereafter, or until I landed at Plymouth, we never were separated for a moment. On the nights that the smoking room was closed for a bit of airing Finnigan and I, being the last to be thrown out, always got sleeping places on deck closest to the smoking-room entrance and slept there, Finnigan athwart the starboard sill and I athwart the port.

Consequently we two, of course, always led the port and starboard rushes that converged and met at the bar the moment the smoking-room doors were unlocked for business each morning. Hunger often during the week drove even the most patient standees behind us to the dining saloon, but never Finnigan and me. Finnigan and I were content with the bar sandwiches. Munching between drafts day after day, we two settled question after question of love and life and death. The old, old days were back again.

When Is A Cruise Passenger Like A Baked Potato?

That man was a poor judge who said a ship is the best place to betray one's true character. The only things that can be seen better at sea than on land are salt water and baked potatoes. A baked potato, at sea, has more character than a dozen inanimate passengers. It is really lovable, and seems to have as much affinity for a landsman as a pea-jacket for a midshipman. But more characterless things than a steamer full of passengers are not to be found except in James' novels: they differ only by nationalities. Frenchmen talk all day, and do nothing; Englishmen eat all day, and say nothing; Spaniards eat nothing, and say nothing; they are the atrabilious favorites of Neptune; Americans drink and smoke all day.
— *W. Wright, 1887.*

❧Fun and Games

❧*Eating, and drinking if you're sober enough to realize it, can get boring after a while. You need to get up and walk it off. But when you do, all you see around you is action, people swimming and running and playing games. Suddenly, you too want action, movement (other than the ship's), a test of your skills. Waiting for you on board is a host of sports you'd never be able to play (or admit to playing) on land: quoits, shuffleboard, ping-pong (which, James Thurber has suggested, should be spelled backwards to better approximate the sound of a game in progress). And then, of course, there's poker, the one game humorists take seriously. Forget those overbuilt phys-ed instructors and listen to humorists Richard Gordon, Petroleum V. Nasby (David R. Locke), James Thurber, and Franklin P. Adams, all of them experts on making anything fun and games.*

Richard Gordon
Salt-Water Hikers, Etc. 1967

SPORTY-MINDED travellers, intending to spread their fifty pounds as thinly as possible over the earth's surface this summer by taking a cruise, can pack their games kit in confidence that most of their favourite pastimes will be available afloat. The equipment is generally fashioned from traditional nautical furnishings, with the same charming ingenuity as ships' funerals are conducted with canvas and twine, weighty fire-bars, and a well sandpapered hatch cover. *Tennis* can for instance be adapted for any reasonably sized square of deck, using a net made from a cargo-hoist and quoits from tarred rope in canvas jackets. The scoring follows lawn tennis, the rules are simple, and can vary with the whim of the captain. *It should never be attempted by anyone over the age of thirty.*

This warning is needed through the peculiar social structure of life on shipboard, a grasp of which can reduce the risk of physical and mental injury to the gamesplayer.

Going to sea, like going to Heaven, gives everyone a fresh start. The landlubberly past drops as swiftly from memory as the disappearing coastline. Social position ashore becomes meaningless in an autocracy where the captain represents, as occasion demands, the Queen, the Law, and the Established Church. Even clothes carry no distinction, one bikini or pair of shorts much resembling any other. Money is irrelevant, there being nothing to spend it on except gin and haircuts, both of which are very reasonable. A cruise ship is not a means of transport, but a comfortable, well-victualled desert island. Why people will pay heavily to involve themselves in such a primitive society is known only to deep-thinking anthropologists and the advertising executives of shipping lines.

The passengers on a cruise thus face the same situation as so inconvenienced the *Bounty* mutineers on Pitcairn Island. Any females available must be fought for, and the nicer they are the nastier the scrap. Blatant rough-and-tumbles on the boat deck being frowned upon by the authorities, the aggression becomes restricted to the ship's games. I once watched a pair of Tarzans playing the finals of the deck tennis competition, under a blazing sun and the eyes of the sexiest girl aboard, with a ferocity which ended the contest by putting one in the ship's hospital with a suspected fractured ankle, and the other in with a suspected coronary occlusion.

Table-tennis, the rowing machine, the gymnasium fixed bicycle, pillow-fighting on the greasy pole, even bouncing on the trampoline, are similarly abused as primaeval exhibitions of masculine vigour. Even *Walking* is a perilous activity at sea. The knowledge that five times round the promenade deck equals a mile seems to obsess overweight males who ashore wouldn't stroll out to post a letter. Possibly they feel diminished by leaving behind their expensive cars and other status symbols of a bulkier nature, seeking to raise themselves in the eyes of the near-naked female sunbathers with a spectacle of physical endurance. Even in the tropics these salt-water hikers puff round amazing distances, calling loudly at each circuit how they would have progressed from Hyde Park Corner to Woking, and finally collapsing outside Basingstoke.

There are fortunately more peaceful sports aboard for passengers in whom the primitive urge to mate burns less fiercely. Bowls is the game probably most free of sexual undertones. Even in beautifully stabilised ships this pastime must be adapted as *Shuffleboard,* in which players armed with poles send small wooden disks scraping several yards down the deck. Passengers liable to insomnia are wise to discover before sailing if their cabin happens to be directly underneath.

Cricket at sea retains an unsullied gentlemanliness. It is played with a light plastic ball on the boat deck, the batsman's strokes severely restricted to the on- or off-side depending in which direction he is likely to give a catch to the mermaids. Sailors are remarkably keen cricket followers, despite spending most of their lives several thousand miles from the nearest blade of grass. In some of their cabins you can find enough equipment for a Test team, they oil their bats lovingly, and appear on deck in the evenings with flannels, pads, and cap to practise cuts and drives against invisible bowlers.

A ship's cricket team is welcomed by the British colony of outlandish places with the pathetic nostalgia they keep for steak-and-kidney pudding, fogs, and even, after a long enough exile, for the Commissioners of Inland Revenue. I once played a match in the middle of the Brazilian jungle at Manaos, a thousand miles up the River Amazon. The stumps we hammered into the baked mud were immovable even by the fastest bowler, there were snakes at long leg, third man was nearly eaten by a jaguar, and all of us were nearly eaten by insects. But to our local compatriots, it was the Test at Lord's and the Oval combined.

Horse Racing is much pleasanter at sea than ashore. Despite the absence of turf, grandstands, and the like, it is free from rain, traffic-jams, queueing for drinks, and those tedious waits between the action. A meeting is held most evenings in the smoke room, the purser rattling the dice and calling the numbers, in obedience to which half-a-dozen pretty girls in jockey caps move wooden horses down a long numbered strip of baize. Betting is on the tote system, and ten per cent is always deducted for seamen's charities. A further ten per cent is also deducted for the purser's savings, another for the head barman (who is entitled to a cut of everything below decks), another for the head steward to keep his mouth shut, and another for his mate to see he does. The steward presenting the winnings on a tray expects a tip, and it is etiquette to spend them on drinks all round.

Our great national game of *Bingo* was probably played at sea in the days of sail. There is also a daily pool on the ship's run, but never bet on "The Captain's Number" — his estimation of the ship's position is invariably so wildly out as to cast suspicions on arrival at Sydney rather than Southampton.

Water Sports are understandably popular at sea, particularly the rite of *Crossing the Line*. In this ancient and witty ceremony, all passengers facing their first change of hemisphere are led out to the swimming pool, fixed in a chair, lathered with porridge and whitewash by the Demon Barber ("Dan Druff"), dosed by the Demon Doctor with an evil mixture concocted by the ship's surgeon (which he hopes nervously is reasonably harmless), then tipped backwards and held under water by strapping young men to the point of asphyxia. The fun generally leaves a burst blood-vessel or two, assorted bruises, and an occasional fracture, and is widely advertised by some shipping lines as the top diversion of the voyage.

A catalogue of ship's sports is incomplete without *Boat Drill*. This occurs precisely at four on Thursday afternoons, anticipated by the passengers as a break in the week's routine comparable with the Saturday soccer match at home. The whistle blows, the passengers don their bulky life-jackets, then make calmly and purposefully towards their boat stations. It is heartening to observe from the disciplined ranks how heavily our glorious traditions of the sea weigh upon us. Only in a British ship — with one or two regrettable exceptions like the *Titanic*— can the players feel certain of all rules being strictly observed, with women and children first and no dirty in-fighting or fouls in the scrum. Foreigners may nowadays beat us at everything else, but it is proud to reflect that at a really satisfactory shipwreck no one in the world can touch us.

Aboard a cargo boat, with less space and no girls, recreations must be largely restricted to the imagination. Sailors are keen subscribers to correspondence courses on subjects like farming, in the mind growing crops and mating bulls, or breeding mental roses and climbing mental mountains. Sadly, nobody in a cargo vessel seems to take the lead in organizing games, or even regular exercise. There is absolutely nothing to do with the long, slowly chugging days across the ocean, except to find a comfortable deck chair and sleep undisturbed in the sun.

Petroleum V. Nasby
The Beauty of Shuffleboard 1882

A PORTION of the passengers, including the English dominie, played a game called "shuffle-board." Squares were marked upon the deck, which were numbered from one to seven. Then some distance from the squares a line was drawn, and what you had to do was to take an implement shaped like a crutch, and shove discs of wood at the squares. We all played it, sooner or later, for on shipboard one will get, in time, to playing pin alone in his room. The beauty about shuffle-board is, one player is as good as another, if not better, for there isn't the slightest skill to be displayed in it. Indeed, the best playing is always done at first, when the player shoots entirely at random. There is a chance that he will strike a square, then; but when one gets to calculating distances, and looking knowingly, and attempting some particular square, the chances are even that the disc goes overboard.

However, it is a good and useful game. The young ladies look well handling the clumsy cues, and the attitudes they are compelled to take are graceful. Then as the vessel lurches they fall naturally in your arms. By the way, it is a curious fact and one worthy of record, that I did not see a young lady fall into the arms of another young lady during the entire voyage.

James Thurber
Speaking of Ping-Pong 1953

I F you have gone on a cruise to relax, and you don't want to romp, run, race or wrassle, stay away from the sports director, a big, energetic blond young man carrying a medicine ball. The female of this species, the sports directress, is active, alert, athletic, aggressive and capable of throwing your wife, or you, over her shoulder with her left hand. If you are not in training and under twenty-eight, don't monkey around with these two. They will run you ragged. They love squatting exercises, chinning themselves, holding their breath, standing on their hands, and touching the deck two thousand times with their finger tips, without bending their knees. Don't try to keep up with them. Refuse their challenges, ignore their taunts. You can't beat them at anything from squatting to ping-pong, unless you are young Mathias, the decathlon champion, and you probably aren't. The sports directors are supposed to organize group recreational activities. This is both a fact and a warning.

Speaking of ping-pong, I once entered a table-tennis tournament aboard the S.S. *President Garfield,* on a trip from New York through the Canal to Los Angeles. The sports director was determined to get me into the table-tennis tournament, probably because he wanted to see me humiliated in the finals. And he did. I lost two straight games to a pretty, attractive young lady, twenty years my junior. The table was too short, the net was too high, the rackets were warped, the ship rocked, a small boy among the spectators began riding me and I got something in my eye. I explained to my opponent after the match that, on land and under fair and reasonable conditions, I could have pinned her ears back, the best day she ever saw. She was honest enough to admit this. A very pleasant girl, and the luckiest woman I have ever met on sea or land.

Franklin P. Adams
A Not Too Deep Sea Chantey 1923

> Then it's O to be on the salty sea with
> the breeze abaft my cheek!
> And it's O for the sport of the wind
> aport (or a-lee) for about a week!
> As the passengers walk on the deck and
> talk of matters wild or tame,
> And seven or eight of us fool with fate
> in a seven-day poker game!

Bed On Board

*T*he *Arundel Castle* is the finest boat I have seen in these seas. She is thoroughly modern, and that statement covers a great deal of ground. She has the usual defect, the common defect, the universal defect, the defect that has never been missing from any ship that ever sailed — she has imperfect beds. Many ships have good beds, but no ship has *very* good ones. In the matter of beds all ships have been badly edited, ignorantly edited, from the beginning. The selection of the beds is given to some hearty, strong-backed, self-made man, when it ought to be given to a frail woman accustomed from girlhood to backaches and insomnia. In Noah's Ark the beds were simply scandalous. Noah set the fashion, and it will endure in one degree of modification or another till the next flood.
— *Mark Twain, 1897.*

"*I suppose Conrad is one of your favorites.*"

Drawing by C. W. Anderson;
© 1933, 1961 The New Yorker Magazine, Inc.

❧Reading and Writing

❧*Much effort and creativity have been expended to adapt land games to the sea, but there is something special about those activities native to the ocean cruise and indispensable to getting away from it all, such as reading and 'riting ('rithmetic is okay, too, if you're into astronomy and word problems using knots). Like the cruise, reading and writing are sedentary, nearly prehistoric pleasures. Humorists Robert Benchley and Jean Kerr have suggestions on what to read (besides this book, of course), and Mark Twain and S. G. Bayne advise you what to write, or at least what not to write.*

Robert Benchley
What to Read at Sea
— If Anything 1930

THE choice of books for whiling away the time on an ocean voyage is a question to which considerable thought should be given. One shouldn't rush off with the first three books that happen to be lying on the library-table as one leaves for the boat, neither should one rely on the generosity of friends to supply one with reading matter for the trip across. For no matter how many people send books to the boat, you are quite sure to find, on settling down to read the next day, that they are all copies of the same one. I think that book-store clerks do it on purpose.

An ocean voyage is a good time not only to get in a little light reading but to catch up with some of the books you never have quite got around to wading through on shore. So I would recommend, in addition to the current fiction success and the latest humorous "steamer-book," of which you will have five copies each given to you, taking a copy of "The Life of Lord Morley" or "Aspects of International Diplomacy" or something good and meaty to give balance to your mental diet. You *might* read a couple of pages in one of them, who can tell?

On the first day out you will appear with three books under your arm and settle down in your chair. You bring three in case you finish one very quickly. It would be such a nuisance to have to keep running down to your cabin for fresh books as fast as you finish one. You wouldn't be surprised if you finished all three before lunch. So you begin on the popular fiction work.

The first page is easy-going and in no time you are on page 2. Then something happens. You take a look at the ocean as you turn the page. It is a funny thing about the ocean. Nobody ever took a quick look at it and turned right away again. You always look a little longer than you intended to. It isn't that you *see* anything. The waves all look alike and follow each other with considerable regularity. But they have a hypnotic quality which makes it possible to look at them for hours at a time without any good excuse. It is maybe five minutes before you get back to page 2 again.

Page 2 suddenly presents tremendous difficulties. You can't seem to get into it. There is too much type, in the first place, and somehow the author doesn't seem to have caught the knack of holding your attention. Before you know it your eyes are back on the ocean again, watching with fascination a slight dipping of the horizon along the top of the rail. It's a funny thing, the ocean. All that water.

But come, come! This isn't reading! Let's skip page 2 and get over on to page 3. That's better. A lot of conversation. Not very good conversation though. Let's see. " 'I am glad that you told me this before I had a chance to fall in love with you,' said Eunice, holding her spoon gingerly poised above her cup." Who was that who just walked past on the deck? You look up to see, although you are sure it was no one you know, and on the way back to page 3 your eyes get caught in the ocean again. Five more minutes out.

"The Life of Lord Morley" has slipped off your lap onto the deck, but somehow that doesn't make much difference. The current fiction success has your forefinger inserted between pages 2 and 3, but otherwise your contact with it has been broken. You have frankly given yourself over to an intense contemplation of the sea and a half-hearted examination of everyone that walks past. You will do this for ten more minutes, you say to yourself, and then go back to your book. Perhaps "The Life of Lord Morley" would be good for a change. This fiction thing seems to be rather footless.

But before you have got around to opening "The Life of Lord Morley" the stewards have come around with bouillon and some of those hearty German sandwiches and there isn't much else to do but stack your three books up very neatly beside your chair and give yourself over to nourishment. A man has got to look out for his health, after all. And then, after eating, he certainly ought to take a turn around the deck or perhaps play a game of deck-tennis. He can't sit in his chair *all* day.

And here is where the books really fulfill their purpose. As they lie on the empty chair, waiting for their owner to come back to read them, they are the object of curious scrutiny by people walking by and those in neighboring chairs. There is always a great interest displayed by passengers in what their fellows are reading—or leaving lying around on their chairs. People in the next chairs will walk past, tipping their heads to one side to see what the title of the book is, and, if they are sure that the owner is on another deck, will even take the book up and thumb its pages. And from these books they judge the occupant of the chair.

Now, since it is pretty well understood that, so long as the ocean presents its distractions and so long as people keep walking past, you are not going to get much further than page 4 in any book you may take out on deck, you might as well get credit among your neighbors for being an important person mentally. Don't leave a paper-covered copy of an Edgar Wallace book lying about. Pick a good one that will look impressive. I used a copy of "The Masters of Modern French Criticism" on my last trip and got quite a name for myself with it. I got about two pages read, but all the people on my side of the ship had me sized up as a serious thinker. Everything went all right until one night a man came up to me and said "I see you are reading Professor Babbitt's book on French Criticism. I would be interested to know what you think of it. I wrote a review of it for the *Nation* when it came out and I wonder if you find the same fault with it that I do." So I had to say that I really had just begun it (he must have seen it lying around for five days) and that I hadn't really formed any opinion on it yet. Eventually, I had to read the book in my berth at night, for he wouldn't let me go.

So it would be well to pick even more esoteric works than that, in order not to get caught by someone who has already read them. The main point is, in all ocean reading, to take books which you don't have to read yourself.

Jean Kerr
Things to Read in the Cabin 1970

M OST people embarking on an ocean voyage bring along a book they've intended to read forever, like *Martin Chuzzlewit* or *The Education of Henry Adams*. I don't find this necessary because (a) I never intend to read *The Education of Henry Adams,* and (b) I find so many interesting things to read right there in the cabin. First, there is this little booklet full of tantalizing information about the ship. You will learn that the keel was laid in Genoa in 1962 (which, I am sure, was a vintage year for keels). In addition, I find it reassuring to learn that the ship is equipped with "Denny-Brown stabilizers with four automatic fins." That sounds about right to me. Six would probably be too many. And, while I don't happen to know anything about the Denny-Brown people, I'm sure they're the best. There is, however, one instruction that always disturbs me. It reads: "Anyone seeing a man falling overboard should shout MAN OVERBOARD STARBOARD or PORT SIDE (Starboard or Port is referred to the right or left of a man facing forward to the bow). Whosoever should hear the call should repeat it loudly and attempt to pass it to the Bridge."

I can't figure that out right this minute, when I have all the time in the world. In an emergency, heavens knows what I'd say. I mean, I know the difference between right and left, but I don't always know where the bow is. As a result, I simply never go on deck unless I am sure that there are a number of responsible people about. I can always put in time in my cabin studying my bilingual dictionary, especially the section marked "Phrases Most Often Used." Others have observed that the authors of these dictionaries do not seem to have a firm grasp of colloquial English. I want to say I am more struck by the fact that they can't seem to get through a page without foreseeing disaster. An air of doom prevails. After intense study, and only a little Dramamine, I am now able to say in flawless Italian, "Conductor, I have experienced misfortunes with my luggage," "Quick, summon a physician, my husband appears to ail," and (my favorite) "Mistress, this plumbing is imperfect and I am unable to bathe."

Another bonus for readers is the Program for the Day, which is slipped under the door each morning. This not only gives you the times of the meals and the titles of the movies but goes on to reveal the wealth of other goodies that await you. "Eleven-thirty: Organ

Recital in the Bamboo Lounge. Tunes from Yesteryear." (Okay, but think about it: it's better than tunes from *this* year.) "Three-thirty: Complimentary Dance Lesson on the Main Deck with Florio and Janet, weather permitting." I happen to feel that this "weather permitting" merely injects an empty note of pessimism, but I suppose you can't have people frugging right over the rails.

The best thing of all, though, is the ship's daily newspaper. This is the absolutely ideal publication. It's as peaceful as a Zen garden. No screaming headlines to ruin your breakfast and make you wonder if you shouldn't take the younger children and move to New Zealand. No headlines at all. The news, if any, will be found underneath a perfume advertisement in very small type. Sometimes it's no more than two or three sentences, and, with any luck at all, you could miss it entirely.

The rest of the paper, however, will be filled with nourishing tidbits. Just last summer I came across a splendid piece that ran under the caption: "Not All Beavers Industrious."

It appears that someone had spent a great deal of time in a beaver community, along with the beavers, trying to discover just how busy they really were. And he did come upon a certain number of upright, responsible beavers who got to the dam on time. On the other hand, there are beavers who loll around day and never get to the dam at all. And, when they do, they have a couldn't-care-less attitude. They chew indifferently on the wrong kind of twigs and slap mud around carelessly, while taking frequent cat-naps or beaver-naps. They have no group spirit and their work is messy. Nowadays, when I loll around, I comfort myself with the thought that I'm just as busy as your average beaver.

Mark Twain
Keeping a Journal 1869

BY 7 o'clock in the evening, dinner was about over; an hour's promenade on the upper deck followed; then the gong sounded and a large majority of the party repaired to the after cabin (upper), a handsome saloon fifty or sixty feet long, for prayers. The unregenerated called this saloon the "Synagogue." The devotions consisted only of two hymns from the "Plymouth Collection," and a short prayer, and seldom occupied more than fifteen minutes. The hymns were accompanied by parlor organ music when the sea was smooth enough to allow a performer to sit at the instrument without being lashed to his chair.

After prayers the Synagogue shortly took the semblance of a writing-school. The like of that picture was never seen in a ship before. Behind the long dining-tables on either side of the saloon, and scattered from one end to the other of the latter, some twenty or thirty gentlemen and ladies sat them down under the swaying lamps, and for two or three hours wrote diligently in their journals. Alas! that journals so voluminously begun should come to so lame and impotent a conclusion as most of them did! I doubt if there is a single pilgrim of all that host but can show a hundred fair pages of journal concerning the first twenty days' voyaging in the Quaker City; and I am morally certain that not ten of the party can show twenty pages of journal for the succeeding twenty thousand miles of voyaging! At certain periods it becomes the dearest ambition of a man to keep a faithful record of his performances in a book; and he dashes at this work with an enthusiasm that imposes on him the notion that keeping a journal is the veriest pastime in the world, and the pleasantest. But if he only lives twenty-one days, he will find out that only those rare natures that are made up of pluck, endurance, devotion to duty for duty's sake, and invincible determination, may hope to venture upon so tremendous an enterprise as the keeping of a journal and not sustain a shameful defeat.

One of our favorite youths, Jack, a splendid young fellow with a head full of good sense, and a pair of legs that were a wonder to look upon in the way of length, and straightness, and slimness, used to report progress every morning in the most glowing and spirited way, and say:

"Oh, I'm coming along bully!" (he was a little given to slang, in his happier moods,) "I wrote ten pages in my journal last night — and you know I wrote nine the night before, and twelve the night before that. Why it's only fun!"

"What do you find to put in it, Jack?"

"Oh, every thing. Latitude and longitude, noon every day; and how many miles we made last twenty-four hours; and all the domino-games I beat, and horse-billiards; and whales and sharks and porpoises; and the text of the sermon, Sundays; (because that'll tell at home, you know,) and the ships we saluted and what nation they were; and which way the wind was, and whether there was a heavy sea, and what sail we carried, though we don't ever carry any, principally, going against a head wind always — wonder what is the reason of that? — and how many lies Moult has told — Oh, every thing! I've got every thing down. My father told me to keep that journal.

Father wouldn't take a thousand dollars for it when I get it done."

"No, Jack; it will be worth more than a thousand dollars — when you get it done."

"Do you? — no, but do you think it will, though?"

"Yes, it will be worth at least as much as a thousand dollars — when you get it done. May be, more."

"Well, I about half think so, myself. It ain't no slouch of a journal."

But it shortly became a most lamentable "slouch of a journal." One night in Paris, after a hard day's toil in sight-seeing, I said:

"Now I'll go and stroll around the cafés awhile, Jack, and give you a chance to write up your journal, old fellow."

His countenance lost its fire. He said:

"Well, no, you needn't mind. I think I won't run that journal any more. It is awful tedious. Do you know — I reckon I'm as much as four thousand pages behind hand. I haven't got any France in it at all. First I thought I'd leave France out and start fresh. But that wouldn't do, *would* it? The governor would say, 'Hello, here — didn't see any thing in France?' *That* cat wouldn't fight, you know. First I thought I'd copy France out of the guide-book, like old Badger in the for'rard cabin who's writing a book, but there's more than three hundred pages of it. Oh, I don't think a journal's any use — do you? They're only a bother, *ain't* they?"

"Yes, a journal that is incomplete isn't of much use, but a journal properly kept, is worth a thousand dollars, — when you've got it done."

"A thousand! — well I should think so. I wouldn't finish it for a million."

His experience was only the experience of the majority of that industrious night-school in the cabin. If you wish to inflict a heartless and malignant punishment upon a young person, pledge him to keep a journal a year.

S. G. Bayne
Post Card Mania 1909

Now we reach the post-card mania. This is the most pernicious disease that has ever seized humanity since the days of the Garden of Eden, and in no better place can it be seen at its worst than on a steamer calling at foreign ports: once it gets a foothold it supplants almost all other vices and becomes a veritable Frankenstein. It is harder to break away from this habit than from poker, gossiping, strong drink, tobacco, or even eating peas with your knife if you have been brought up that way. The majority of the "Corks" when landing at a port would not have stopped to say "Good morning" to Adam, to take a peep at Bwana Tumbo's hides and horns, or to pick up the Declaration of Independence if it lay at their feet — in their eager rush to load up with the cards necessary to let all their friends know that they had arrived at any given place on the map. This is but the first act in the drama, for stamps must be found, writing places must be secured, pencils, pens and ink must be had, together with a mailing list as long as to-day and to-morrow. The smoking-room is invaded, the lounge occupied, and every table, desk and chair in the writing-room is preempted, to the exclusion of all who are not addressing post-cards. Although we toiled like electrified beavers we got behind on the schedule, so that those who did not finish at Malta had to work hard to get their cards off at Constantinople, and so on through the trip. The chariot of Aurora would hardly hold their output at a single port. At the start it was a mild, pleasurable fad, but later it absorbed the victim's mind to such an extent that he thought of nothing but the licking of stamps and mailing of cards to friends — who get so many of them that they are for the most part considered a nuisance and after a hasty glance are quietly dropped in the waste-basket. Many had such an extensive collection of mailing lists that it became necessary to segregate them into divisions; in some cases these last were labeled for classification, "Atlantic Coast Line," "Middle West," "Canadian Provinces," "New England," "Europe," etc. Again they were subdivided into trades and professions, such as lawyers, ministers, politicians, stock brokers, real estate agents, bankers (in jail and out of it), dermatologists and "hoss-doctors." This habit obtained such a hold on people who were otherwise respectable that they would enter into any "fake," to gratify their obsession. Some of the "Corks" did not tour Spain but remained on the ship; many of these would get up packages of cards, dating them as if at Cadiz, Seville or Granada, and request those who were landing to mail them at the proper places, so as to impose on their friends at home. I felt no hesitancy, after silently receiving my share of this fraud, in quietly dropping them overboard as a just punishment for this impertinence. Incidents like this will account in part for the non-delivery of post-cards and the disappointment of those who did not receive them.

Our Purser had what is known in tonsorial cirlces as a "walrus" or drooping moustache; he was plied with so many foolish questions in regard to this mailing business that he became very nervous and tugged vigorously at this ornament whenever something new was sprung on him. It is said that water will wear a hole in stone, and so it came to pass that he pulled his moustache out, hair by hair, till there were left only nine on a side. The style of his adornment was then necessarily changed to the "baseball," by which it was known to the "fans" on board.

The handling of this enormous output has already become an international postal problem of grave importance in many countries; the mails have been congested and demoralized, and thousands of important letters have been delayed because Mrs. Galley-West would have her friends on Riverside Drive thoroughly realize that she has got as far as Queenstown on her triumphal tour, and that she and all the little Galley-Wests are "feeling quite well, I thank you."

The ultimate fate of the post-card mania is as yet undecided. It may, like the measles or the South Sea Bubble, run its course and that will end it; on the other hand, it may grow to such proportions that it will shut out all human endeavor and bring commercial pursuits to a complete standstill.

Junk

This is a portrait of Souvenir Sue
　Who whether in Brooklyn or Rome
Must always find something to break off and snatch
　To label and carry back home!

❧Shore Excursions

❧*The most strenuous activity on a cruise is getting off the ship, away from the luxuries and the now familiar rocking of the . . . I almost said cradle. Yet many cruise passengers look forward to each excursion; they go to their chosen surrogate crow's-nests and try to be the first to sight the next island, like a Columbus, a Gulliver, or a Peeping Tom. Here are the experiences of three humorous travel writers with various aspects of the shore excursion in various parts of the world.*

S. J. Perelman
Hell-Bent on Kultur: Turkey 1977

THE portents were disquieting. Frogmen had discovered a leak in the S.S. *Iskanderun* — or perhaps in its captain, my knowledge of Turkish was rudimentary — and marine urologists doubted if either could be made seaworthy by departure time. Her sister ship, the *Ankara*, had been pressed into service instead, but she was fully booked, though a remote possibility existed that a bed might be installed for me in the chain locker. In this my darkest hour, a fat angel miraculously appeared and with a wave of her wand dispersed the haze of bureaucracy. Roxana, whose plump beauty recalled those massive favorites of the Ottoman sultans, derived a scanty wage as interpreter for the local bureau of Reuter's. I plied her with quantities of Turkish delight and halvah, and in return she winkled out a first-class cabin for me on the *Ankara*. I shall never forget her great mascara-trimmed eyes, awash in carbohydrates, bidding me farewell as we steamed out of the Golden Horn.

My fellow-passengers aboard the *Ankara* — originally a U.S. Coast Guard hospital ship named *Solace* and refitted for the Turkish holiday trade — were pretty much what one would encounter on a Caribbean pleasure cruise, a mixture of businessmen and professionals bound for the resorts dotting the Turquoise Coast. At the outset, mealtimes were a vexation to the spirit, inasmuch as my table companions were baffled by every patois I attempted, including Pushtu, Volapük, Esperanto, and even Lenni-Lenape, the argot the Delaware Indians employed in Bucks County. Wearying at length of sign language, I finally got myself transferred to a group that understood English in varying degree. It including a craggy old civil engineer from Oregon, a young American officer and his family stationed at the NATO base in Izmir, a Turkish lady pediatrician who had interned in the States, and an English schoolmaster. Of these, the latter predictably turned out to be the best value; educated at Cambridge, he had known E. M. Forster and Montague Rhodes James, served in Africa and New Guinea as administrator of the British version of our Peace Corps, and taught history at Winchester.

"I say," I remarked to him, indicating several tablefuls of elderly, affluent people festooned with cameras, light meters, and field glasses, whose dialogue crackled with more explosive gutturals than a Wagnerian opera. "Who in the world are they?"

"Instinct should tell you, my dear chap," he replied. "Those are Teutons hell-bent on Kultur. They're all equipped with Baedekers and archaeological surveys of Ephesus, Pergamum, and Halicarnassus, and as we progress from Izmir to Fethiye, Antalya, Alanya, and Mersin, they will swarm off into a series of Mercedes-Benz buses to gobble up the visibly fake antiques planted there by dealers."

His forecast was correct. Whether it was the Teutons' zeal that put me off, or a relapse of the ecclesiastical virus contracted in too many Russian cathedrals, or the stupefying heat, I had no stomach for Greek amphitheaters, and I decided to confine my sightseeing to the towns. Izmir's seafront, its old-fashioned coastal shipping, cafés, and Victorian facades, were delightful, and the variety of wares in its colorful bazaar outstanding. It was astonishing, by the way, to see how inexpensive the ordinary necessities of life were as compared to those in the States. A first-class broom, such as would cost $2.38 in an American supermarket, retailed here for 82 cents. I was strongly tempted to pick up half a dozen as presents for weekend hosts at home, but the complexities of transporting them in my baggage across Asia dissuaded me.

That much said, however, the rest of Izmir's business area, and those in the other ports, was purgatorial, an affliction and a malaise. The Turks have succumbed to the worldwide infatuation with the motor scooter, recklessly dismembering pedestrians and whizzing at breakneck speed through byways designed for the ox cart. What a satisfying assertion of one's virility it is, as the Italians long ago discovered, to gun these fiendish machines, what more convenient outlet for his xenophobia than to spray some hapless foreigner with mud and watch him dive for cover! My experience in Antalya may well be a classic demonstration. As I stood deafened by the clatter of steam hammers demolishing a kiosk in its main street, two Vespas bore down on me from opposite directions. So close did they pass that they sheared off eight buttons from my sleeves (it was, as the knowledgeable will instantly guess, an English jacket). I naturally shook my fist after them and jumped up and down on my hat like Edgar Kennedy, but it availed me naught.

Julia Ward Howe
There's Nothing to See:
The Bahamas 1860

THERE was a sort of eddy at the gangway of our steamer, made by the conflicting tides of those who wanted to come on board and of those who wanted to go on shore. We were among the number of the latter, but were stopped and held by the button by one of the former, while those more impatient or less sympathizing made their way to the small boats which waited below. The individual in question had come alongside in a handsome barge, rowed by a dozen stout blacks, in the undress uniform of the Zouaves. These men, well drilled and disciplined, seemed of a different sort from the sprawling, screaming creatures in the other boats, and their bright red caps and white tunics became them well. But he who now claimed my attention was of British birth and military profession. His face was ardent, his pantaloons were of white flannel, his expression of countenance was that of habitual discontent, but with a twinkle of geniality in the eye which redeemed the Grumbler from the usual tedium of his tribe. He accosted us as follows:

"Go ashore? What for? To see something, eh? There's nothing to see; the island isn't bigger than a nut-shell, and doesn't contain a single prospect. — Go ashore and get some dinner? There isn't anything to eat there. — Fruit? None to speak of; sour oranges and green bananas. — I went to market last Saturday, and bought one cabbage, one banana, and half a pig's head; — there's a market for you! — Fish? Oh, yes, if you like it. — Turtle? Yes, you can get the Gallipagos turtle; it makes tolerable soup, but has not the green fat, which, in my opinion, is the most important feature in turtle-soup. — Shops? You can't buy a pair of scissors on the island, nor a baby's bottle; — broke mine the other day, and tried to replace it; couldn't. — Society? There are lots of people to call upon you, and bore you to death with returning their visits."

At last the Major went below, and we broke away, and were duly conveyed to *terra firma*.

Mark Twain
We Shall Not Go Ashore: Italy 1869

WE reached Leghorn in time to see all we wished to see of it long before the city gates were closed for the evening, and then came on board the ship.

We felt as though we had been away from home an age. We never entirely appreciated, before, what a very pleasant den our state-room is; nor how jolly it is to sit at dinner in one's own seat in one's own cabin, and hold familiar conversation with friends in one's own language. Oh, the rare happiness of comprehending every single word that is said, and knowing that every word one says in return will be understood as well! We would talk ourselves to death, now, only there are only about ten passengers out of the sixty-five to talk to. The others are wandering, we hardly know where. We shall not go ashore in Leghorn. We are surfeited with Italian cities for the present, and much prefer to walk the familiar quarter-deck and view this one from a distance.

Harboring A Cold

There was great ado at starting, and when we finally steamed out of New York harbor past the "Goddess of Liberty" one fine morning, the air was rent with the screeching of steam sirens and the tooting of whistles. The "Goddess" stood calm and silent on her pedestal; she looked virtuous (which was natural to her, being made of metal), but her stoic indifference was somewhat upset by an icy stalactite that hung from her classic nose. One of the passengers remarked that Bartholdi ought to have supplied her with a handkerchief, but this suggestion was considered flippant by his Philistine audience, and it made no impression whatever. — *S. G. Bayne, 1909.*

❧Boredom

❧*Let's face it: when we have nothing we have to do, we tend to do nothing. When we do nothing, we're bored. There's nothing inherently boring about a cruise. It's just that man is not an easily satisfied creature. Why else does he travel? Why else did he invent the weekend?*

Boredom has two stages. First, we lose perspective. What might have fascinated us, what we looked forward to, no longer does. The second step is to let our thoughts run away with us (since we ourselves have nowhere to go but overboard). Humorists, satisfied even less than the average Joe or Jane, love to dwell on what an ocean cruise can do to your mind almost as much as on what it can do to your stomach. Here are selections from the work of such notable travel writers as E. W. Howe and Nicholas Coleridge, who describe the two steps of boredom, and a poem by John Updike, better known for his novels, which introduces us to the most inactive of activities.

John Updike
Shipbored 1958

That line is the horizon line.
The blue above it is divine.
The blue below it is marine.
Sometimes the blue below is green.

Sometimes the blue above is gray,
Betokening a cloudy day.
Sometimes the blue below is white,
Foreshadowing a windy night.

Sometimes a drifting coconut
Or albatross adds color, but

The blue above is mostly blue.
The blue below and I are, too.

E. W. Howe
The Same Old Story 1927

I DOUBT whether anyone on land, who has never gone through with
it, can realize how time lags at sea. You may think you have seen a
weary yawn, but you have not, unless you have seen a man yawn on
the deck of a ship after it has been at sea seven or eight days. On
land, there is always something going on; there may not be much,
but there is something. If you live in town, a man may come in and
tell you that the bridge over Big Creek is out, and that he was compelled to go around six miles in order to get to town. If you live in the
country, a candidate, or the assessor or a traveler, is likely to come
along and tell you something you had not heard; but if you are on a
ship at sea you soon see nothing new, and hear nothing new. There
are the same passengers every day, and the sea soon becomes as uninteresting as the wall-paper in a room you have lived in for months. I
have heard about the changing lights and shadows on the ocean, but
have yet to see them. The men sit around in the smoking-room, and
talk about the same old things: Singapore, Penang, Colombo, Bombay, Calcutta, etc. On the "Siberia" it was Yokohama, Kobe, Hong
Kong, etc. Beyond Bombay it will be Port Said, Suez, Arden, etc.
Occasionally a man tells a story; always a story I have heard.

Nicholas Coleridge
Contemplating Murder 1985

OF all the legs on Phileas Fogg's journey the Pacific scenery can
have changed the least: deep blue water stretching for miles into
the distance and not a sign of life or traffic. The emptiness was awe-
some. For hours we stared over the rail looking for evidence of progress. Did the sea become less black as we steamed further from
Japan, or was this an early warning of sea blindness? On the afternoon of the fourth day we passed another ship, a Russian trawler,
and elbowed each other out of the way in our haste to take a look.

The following morning we saw a seagull — a black-beaked Goony
Bird from Midway Island — and it monopolised conversation for the
day. You would be surprised how much mileage you can wring out of

a seagull, by the time you've discussed its wingspan, feeding habits, migration, danger from oil slicks and a dozen other aspects besides.

We passengers were ingenious in our efforts to occupy ourselves. No avenue was left unexplored in making our own entertainment. Some days we played golf on the deck with imaginary balls and clubs. "Great shot Erwin, straight into the bunker."

One Californian stood on the fo'c'sle completing a cyclorama of photographs of the view through 360°. He was confident it would be endlessly diverting for his neighbours back home in Oakland to see thirty-six frames of the blue horizon.

After dinner we curled up in the saloon like boa constrictors digesting a bellyful of cholesterol. At a card table in the corner, illuminated by a low wattage overhead light, a gentle game of picquet was in progress. On a sofa a fluffy-haired matron appliqued a pincushion with the legend "Louise will make a House a Home". In all probability this was Miss Jane Marple, taking time out from an Agatha Christie thriller.

There can't have been a person on board who didn't contemplate murder just to break the routine. Motive: cold-blooded boredom. All we needed was the victim. There were eight candidates, each one of them spoiling for a fatal dash of spiked tabasco in their Bloody Mary.

VICTIM A: Marcie, 56, a widow from San Diego. Collects Chinese carpets and Tiffany stained glass. Recently retired from her job as senior vice-president for personnel in a major insurance corporation. Spent several months in Nasser's Egypt in 1957. Latent Islamic sympathies.

VICTIM B: Bob, 62, from Los Angeles. Works on the management side of an aerospace company. Served at Arnheim in the Second World War, later spending some time as a prisoner of war. Firm fan of the Syndicated Columnist Andy Rooney.

VICTIM C: Bob's wife Mary, 60ish. Drinks Budweiser lager and favours electric blue trouser suits. On a previous cruise was once invited to a cocktail party by an English Duke and Duchess. Claims not to recall their names and to have found them snooty.

VICTIM D: Mary's sister May, 58. White-haired and kittenish. Innocuous personality masks ruthless hand at picquet.

VICTIM E: May's corpulent husband Bill, 61. Works in same aerospace outfit as his brother-in-law. Brooding and silent. Possibly hot-tempered when roused. Never seen without his baseball cap.

VICTIM F: Charlotte, 45, married to the ship's radio officer. Once spent a week in London on an American Express package tour and found herself sitting next to her son's orthodontist at the Shaftesbury Theatre. Has since been convinced of the smallness of the world.

VICTIM G: Japanese student, 21, with unpronounceable name. Embarking on a round the world tour with $6,500 in travellers cheques to last him a year. Shaky English. Points at items on the menu at random. Often eats tinned pears with dill pickles off the same plate.

VICTIM H: Subversive English writer in panama hat. Sometimes scribbles a snatch of conversation on the cuff of his shirt. Otherwise immersed for long periods in the National Geographic, perusing fascinating articles on Canadian wheat farming.

Neptune, Wordsworth, And Bach

I know nothing so tedious and exasperating as that regular slap of the wilted sails when the ship rises and falls with the slow breathing of the sleeping sea, one greasy, brassy swell following another, slow, smooth, immitigable as the series of Wordsworth's "Ecclesiastical Sonnets." Even at his best, Neptune, in a *tête-à-tête,* has a way of repeating himself, an obtuseness to the *ne quid nimis,* that is stupefying. It reminds me of organ-music and my good friend Sebastian Bach. A fugue or two will do very well; but a concert made up of nothing else is altogether too epic for me. There is nothing so desperately monotonous as the sea, and I no longer wonder at the cruelty of pirates. — *James Russell Lowell, 1876.*

"*Good Lord, no. My husband and I come cruising every year. Isn't that right, steward?*"

❧Lovemaking

❧*When you feel like doing nothing and boredom seems to be reaching Step Two, you can always turn to the person next to you and talk about the weather, while taking in his or her attractions. For many passengers, such conversation is the heart of their journey. Nowhere since college dorm-life has it been so convenient to really get to know people, and so difficult to hide a thing. Humorist and traveler extraordinaire Robert Benchley provides excellent advice for the passenger who seeks pure peace and quiet — well, almost. Then Rudyard Kipling has a few lines on love aboard ship.*

Robert Benchley
Traveling in Peace *c.1924*

EVEN in an off year, the conversational voltage is very high on the trans-Atlantic greyhounds (ocean liners). There is something in the sea air which seems to bring a sort of kelp to the surface even in the most reticent of passengers, and before the ship has passed Fire Island you will have heard as much dull talk as you would get at a dozen Kiwanis meetings at home. And the chances are that you, yourself, will have done nothing that you can be particularly proud of as a raconteur. They tell me that there is something that comes up from the bilge which makes people like that on shipboard.

I myself solved the problem of shipboard conversation by traveling alone and pretending to be a deaf-mute. I recommend this ruse to other irritable souls.

There is no sense in trying to effect it if you have the family along. There is no sense in trying to effect *anything* if you have the family along. But there is something about a family man which seems to attract prospective talkers. Either the Little Woman scrapes up acquaintances who have to have their chairs moved next to yours and tell you all about how rainy it was all spring in East Orange, or the children stop people on the deck and drag them up to you to have you show them how to make four squares out of six matches, and once you have established these contacts, you might as well stay in your stateroom for the rest of the voyage.

Once you are alone, you can then start in on the deaf-mute game. When you go down to dinner, write out your order to the steward and pretty soon the rest of the people at your table will catch on to the fact that something is wrong. You can do a few pleasant passes of sign language if the thing seems to be getting over too slowly. As a matter of fact, once you have taken your seat without remarking on the condition of the ocean to your right-hand neighbor, you will have established yourself as sufficiently queer to be known as "that man at our table who can't talk." Then you probably will be left severely alone.

Once you are out on deck, stand against the rail and look off at the horizon. This is an invitation which few ocean-talkers can resist. Once they see anyone who looks as if he wanted to be alone, they immediately are rarin' to go. One of them will come up to you and look at the horizon with you for a minute, and then will say:

"Isn't that a porpoise off there?"

If you are not very careful you will slip and say:

"Where?" This is fatal. What you should do is turn and smile very sweetly and nod your head as if to say: "Don't waste your time, neighbor. I can't hear a word you say." Of course, there is no porpoise and the man never thought there was; so he will immediately drop that subject and ask you if you are deaf. Here is where you may pull another bone. You may answer: "Yes, very." That will get you nowhere, for if he thinks that he can make you hear by shouting, he will shout. It doesn't make any difference to him what he has to do to engage you in conversation. He will do it. He would spell words out to you with alphabet blocks if he thought he could get you to pay any attention to his story of why he left Dallas and what he is going to do when he gets to Paris.

So keep your wits about you and be just the deafest man that ever stepped foot on a ship. Pretty soon he will get discouraged and will pass on to the next person he sees leaning over the rail and ask *him* if that isn't a "porpoise 'way off there." You will hear the poor sucker say, "Where?" and then the dam will break. As they walk off together you will hear them telling each other how many miles they get to a gallon and checking up on the comparative sizes of the big department stores in their respective towns.

After a tour of the smoking-room and writing-room making deaf-and-dumb signs to the various stewards, you will have pretty well advertised yourself as a hopeless prospect conversationally. You may then do very much as you like.

Perhaps not quite as you like. There may be one or two slight disadvantages to this plan. There may be one or two people on board to whom you *want* to speak. Suppose, for instance, that you are sitting at one of those chummy writing desks where you look right into the eyes of the person using the other half. And suppose that those eyes turn out to be something elegant; suppose they turn out to be very elegant indeed. What price being dumb then?

Your first inclination, of course, is to lean across the top of the desk and say: "I beg your pardon, but is this your pen that I am using?" or even more exciting: "I beg your pardon, but is this your letter that I am writing?" Having been posing as a deaf-mute up until now, this recourse is denied you, and you will have to use some other artifice.

There is always the old Roman method of writing notes. If you decide on this, just scribble out the following on a bit of ship's stationery: "I may be deaf and I may be dumb, but if you think that makes any difference in the long run, you're crazy." This is sure to attract the lady's attention and give her some indication that you are favorably impressed with her. She may write a note back to you. She may even write a note to the management of the steamship line.

Another good way to call yourself to her attention would be to upset the writing desk. In the general laughter and confusion which would follow, you could grab her and carry her up on deck where you could tell her confidentially that you really were not deaf and dumb but you were just pretending to be that way in order to avoid talking to people who did not interest you. The fact that you were talking to her, you could point out, was a sure sign that she, alone, among all the people on the ship, *did* interest you; a rather pretty compliment to her, in a way. You could then say that, as it was essential that none of the other passengers should know that you could talk, it would be necessary for her to hold conversations with you clandestinely, up on the boat deck, or better yet, in one of the boats. The excitement of this would be sure to appeal to her, and you would unquestionably become fast friends.

There is one other method by which you could catch her favor as you sat looking at her over the top of the desk, a method which is the right of every man whether he be deaf, dumb or bow-legged. You might wink one eye very slowly at her. It wouldn't be long then before you could tell whether or not it would be worth your while to talk.

However it worked out, you would have had a comparatively peaceful voyage.

Rudyard Kipling
Amour de Voyage *c1900*

And I was a man who could write you rhyme
(Just so much for you, nothing more),
And you were the woman I loved for a time —
Loved for a little, and nothing more,
We shall go our ways when the voyage is o'er,
You with your beauty and I with my rhymes,
With a dim remembrance rising at times
(Only a memory, nothing more)
Of a lovely face and some worthless rhymes.

Meantime till our comedy reaches its end
(Its comic ending, and nothing more)
I shall live as your lover who loved as a friend —
Shall swear true love till Life be o'er.
And you, you must make believe and attend,
As the steamer throbs from shore to shore.

And so, we shall pass the time for a little
(Pass it in pleasure, and nothing more),
For vows, alas! are sadly brittle,
And each may forget the oaths that we swore.
And have we not loved for an age, and age?
And was I not yours from shore to shore?
From landing-stage to landing-stage
Did I not worship and kneel and adore?
And what is a month in love but an age?
And who in their senses would wish for more?

Afloat

In the steamer, O my darling! when
   the foghorns scream and blow,
And the footsteps of the steward softly
   come and softly go,
When the passengers are groaning
   with a deep and sincere woe,
Will you think of me and love me, as
   you did not long ago?

In the cabin, O my darling! think not
   bitterly of me,
Though I rushed away and left you in
   the middle of our tea:
I was seized with a sudden longing to
   gaze upon the damp, deep sea —
It was best to leave you then, dear;
   best for you and best for me.
       — *Anonymous*

PEOPLE

Cruisemates

Rube Goldberg and Sam Boal
The Seasoned Traveler
Aboard Ship 1954

THE Seasoned Traveler may be recognized as early in the voyage as the Going-Away Party. The first thing he does is leave his own cabin as quickly as possible. He has no wish to talk to friends who are staying home. (Besides, strangers' parties are more fun.)

After the boat has left the pier, the Seasoned Traveler sniffs the air and says, "My, my! You can just smell it. The sea, of course."

So that the tourist will have no difficulty in assuming the Proper Worldly Look, we present the famous "Six Rules for Seasoned Traveling":

1. Invite no cameraderie with people seated at your table in the dining salon. They will then think you are Important.
2. On the second day out, announce, "Garbo's aboard, you know." Do not amplify this remark.
3. In the event of bad weather, be hearty. Slap sick voyagers on the back and begin circulating rumors that the ship's physician was headed for a brilliant career ashore, but women and drink did him in.
4. When naïve passengers crowd the railings to laugh at porpoises or whales, keep grimly reading your copy of *Black Beauty,* which you must bring along for this purpose.
5. Decline to enter the ship's distance pool, declaring you know for certain that it's fixed.
6. Do not ask the chief engineer to let you see the engine room (because if you ask him, he'll let you).

Talking and flirting with people you've never seen before and will probably never see again — except for that coincidental meeting at some distant outpost, or at the grocery down the street — talking and flirting are wonderful things, but many prefer simply to sit back and watch. In fact, this book has been librotechtonically designed by an international committee of bibliolologists to provide the most effective screen for people-watching known to either man or woman. Will Rogers provides a clear and far-ranging introduction to those you will see on the other side of these pages.

Will Rogers
Life on the Rolling Sea 1934

WELL all I know is just what I read in the papers, or what I see on ship board. A ship is supposed to be a great meeting place or melting pot. The first day everybody walks by kinder acting like they are not paying any attention to each other, the second day they size each other up. The third day after the sizing up they go back to passing without looking, as they did the first day. If by that time you haven't got everybody's number, you are just plain dumb.

There has been enough heads together in the meantime to patch up, or fill in any odds and ends that might be missing about some of 'em. It's awful hard to be on a boat anywhere, and not be recognized by sight by somebody. Then if you have any past, the one that knows it, trades it for something about somebody that they know. Then if there is any missing information you can always go to the purser. There is nobody in America, or the civilized world that a purser on a boat don't know. He makes a hotel clerk look like a man that was deaf, dumb and blind. He has had this or that man on the voyage, away back when they used to have their wife, or husband with 'em. That's how long he knows 'em.

Then to help out your information you have the folks on a boat that do nothing but ride on boats. They will hem you up back over the propeller and tell you how many times they have crossed this particular stretch of ocean. If it's to Honolulu they can point out the various sharks and call 'em by name as they swim along by the boat and beg for an arm or leg.

Then there is always the "Buyers" on there that change clothes a few times a day and make a play for all the women, they are what the old time country drummer was. They know all of Wynn's and Pearl's latest jokes and what the country will come to if they keep on carrying on like they are. Then the girls with all the colored slacks on. It takes an awful rough sea to keep them from walking the deck. And there is many of 'em on that you wouldent hardly call a girl anymore.

Then there is the old grouchy fellows that just grunt if you speak to 'em. And the pleasant old gals that will just tell you right off that this is their first trip, and they are having a great time, and they are going to enjoy it. And they want you to know it. They always know some-body that you know, and you both say, "Ain't the world little after all."

Then there is generally a diplomat of some breed on board. He always looks like a flat-footed secreat police. Because you can tell one a ship's length away. You hem him up in the smoking room and he talks very mysterious about his trip and his mission. He tells you he is being called home for a "consultation," but it's generally for an examination. Then the children "God bless 'em," they are running and tripping over everybody. It takes a rough day to quiet them down. And you almost wish for it. Then there is the fast walker around the deck. They never walk at home, but they are going to be athaletic on this trip.

Oh yes, then the fellow, or fellows with some addresses that they want to give you the minute they find where you are going. "The pro-prietor of the Huey Long Hotel in Noboskoboski, Siberia, is an old friend of ours. He was lovely to us. Give him this card, and he will look after you. He will give you the room with the bath."

Then too there is the exclusive ones. They are on the same boat, but they look on the others as lepers. They don't want to be contami-nated. They look like the minute they get off the boat they will fly to a castle somewhere away from all earthly things. Then there is the ship's officers who are always pleasant and nice. And that must be quite a trial at times, with all the questions that are asked of them. "Officer tell me which is the port and which is the starboard side of this boat, I just can't get it straight, and why in the world do they call 'em by those odd names?"

"Oh Captain, what time will we dock?" "How about my camera, they say these Japs are cranky as goats about taking pictures, I don't see why, every country has blue prints of the others' fortifications."

"How many cigarettes can I take in? Suppose I smoke a little on each one, will that let me in with more?" "No madam, you can take all the butts in you want."

"What does those bells mean ringing all the time, and how in the world do you tell the time by 'em, they all ring alike to me?" "Will they ever get through scrubbing this boat? I guess they are going to keep on till everybody falls." "Why don't they put an outrigger arrangement on this boat like they those kanalas do at Honolulu to keep it from turning over?" "Imagine the little Japanese saying their money is better than ours! Why I give him real money for this hand full of yens." "Officer is it true that the banks in Japan all have Chinese cashiers?" "Well here we are! Do we have to tell these little fellows all about ourselves, and what we got, and why?"

&*Here are a few examples of what sorts of type (or types of sort) you can expect to see (or be, to someone else) on your next voyage. Ask any cruise line. They all guarantee at least twenty real characters per voyage; the better lines even hire from casting agencies to make your trip seem more authentic. You may, in fact, be trying to escape from characters, from the ones you work with or live next to. But characters, as well as stereotypes, are better on a cruise; they're what you always forget: the enjoyable first couple of meetings, before they begin to grate or, in the case of walking stereotypes, before you realize there's nothing else to them. Sit back and let such luminaries as Harriet Beecher Stowe, James Thurber, Ludwig Bemelmans, Irvin S. Cobb, and John Phoenix (G. H. Derby) introduce you to a few.*

James Thurber
Mrs. Abigail Pritchard 1953

IF you travel much on ships you are bound, sooner or later, to run into Mrs. Abigail Pritchard, as I shall call her. She is not just one woman, but many; I have encountered at least fifteen of her. Mrs. Pritchard may be forty-five, or she may be seventy, but her average age, I should say, is about fifty-seven. She comes from Boston, Hartford, Germantown, Syracuse, Toledo, Chicago, Louisville, St. Louis, Denver, Sacramento, and both Portlands. She is a widow, fairly well off, whose children are happily married and the fathers, or mothers, of the prettiest and brightest youngsters in the world, and she has snapshots and anecdotes to prove it. She takes two Daiquiris before dinner and a highball afterwards, and smokes Players, on the ground that they are made of actual tobacco, whereas American cigarettes, in her opinion, are composed of rum, molasses, shredded cork, and factory sweepings. She prefers domestic Burgundies, however, because the so-called French vintages you find on ships are really only cheap Algerian wine that has been poured into genuine bottles labeled Pommard or Chablis. Mrs. Pritchard is full of interesting little anecdotes about the late Sir Harry Oakes, the late Richard Halliburton ("that dear boy"), a Colonel Grosvenor in Penang, the gifted Courtney girls (whoever they are), John Barrymore ("poor old Jack"), Heifetz, Houdini, Nell Brinkley, Anna Eva Fay, Percy Marmont, Maurice Costello ("the king of them all"), Kip Rhinelander, Mrs. O. H. P. Belmont, Struthers Burt, Ky Laffoon and anybody else whose name you happen to mention. Mrs. Pritchard is certain she saw Judge Crater in the Casino at Cannes in 1937, where he was known as Maltby or Goadby, or some such name. "How do you do, Judge Crater?" she said to him firmly. He started — there could be no doubt of that. "My name is Maltby (or Goadby), madam," the man said, and hurried away.

Mrs. Pritchard can invariably spot, aboard ship, professional gamblers, unmarried couples sharing the same stateroom, fugitives from justice, fingermen formerly in the employ of Al Capone, cocaine sniffers, bay-rum drinkers, professional men of dubious integrity, women who are mortally ill but don't know it, unhappy wives and gentlemen with phony foreign accents. It makes you nervous to talk to, or rather listen to, Mrs. Pritchard. You twist restlessly in your chair, confident that she has figured you for an absconder, a black-marketeer, or a white-slave trader. Mrs. Pritchard spends at least two months of every year on ships, but I often wonder why, since she suspects that there is skulduggery afoot from the chartroom to the hold. If the ship is even half an hour late in shoving off, she whispers that "Uncle Joe is behind this delay." She never clears this up, though, but merely shakes her head wisely, if you ask her what she means. She is sure the ship is going to put to sea with broken pumps, insufficient lifeboats, and a typhoid carrier among the crew. Two days out, she tells you she doesn't like the look of the saxophone player's complexion — he has something contagious, mark her words. The third day out she declares that the chief steward is secreting fifteen thousand pounds of roast beef, which he intends to sell to a syndicate in Port-au-Prince. It costs ten thousand dollars a day to operate a ship, she read in the *Reader's Digest,* and this ridiculous amount is due to thefts of supplies by the stewards.

Even the captain of the ship is not above her suspicion. She is positive that he forgot to order all those automobiles in the hold lashed down, and she knows they will roll to one side if a storm comes up, causing the ship to list, like the *Vestris,* and sink. Mrs. Pritchard loves to tell about the time the master of an ocean liner was seized with a heart attack while steering the boat — she still thinks he was an epileptic — and almost ran into an iceberg. But her favorite story is about the time she was on a West Indies cruise, and caught a glimpse of the captain one day. She recognized him instantly as a Major Quantrell (or Chantress, or some such name) wanted in Rangoon for the shooting of a missionary's daughter in a fashionable gambling house. Mrs. Pritchard points out that a captain's cabin is the perfect hide-out for fugitives from justice, since nobody is allowed in the cabin except the officers, and they are probably no better than they ought to be, themselves.

The young traveler will naturally expect old, experienced me to advise him how to avoid, or to deal with, Mrs. Pritchard. Well, you can't avoid her. Just dismiss that from your mind. She pops up from everywhere and out from behind everything. Even if you hid in the engine room, she would search you out. As for dealing with the old girl, I have invented a rather nasty game called Back Her in the Corner, which works wonders.

"You know the Hotel l'Aiglon in Roquebrune, of course?" I say to her, casually.

"To be sure," she replies. "That perfectly gorgeous view of the Bay of Monte Carlo at night!"

We both look dreamy.

"Ah, yes," I sigh, "and those wonderful sardines grilled in triple-sec!"

"Yes, yes," she sighs, "those delicious sardines."

You see, she has to keep up a show of having been every place I have been. And here's where my game gets nasty.

"There isn't any Hotel l'Aiglon in Roquebrune," I say coldly, "and there aren't any sardines grilled in triple-sec."

She is furious. I have tricked her, and hell hath no fury like a woman tricked. She gives me a wide berth after that, not even nodding or smiling when I pass her on deck. I can get away with this little game because I am fifty-six, but such conduct on the part of the *young* traveler would seem imprudent, disrespectful and ill-bred. You'll have to devise your own method of dealing with Mrs. Pritchard. You mustn't expect me to solve all your travel problems. And please don't write and ask me what to do in the event that you run into the gifted Courtney sisters. I simply do not know.

John Phoenix
Tramp! Tramp! Tramp! 1855

WE had a glorious day aboard the old *Northerner;* we played whist, and sang songs, and told stories, many of which were coeval with our ancient school-lessons, and, like them, came very easy, going over the second time, and many drank strong waters, and becoming mopsed thereon, toasted "the girls we'd left behind us," whereat one, who, being a temperance man, had guzzled soda-water until his eyes seemed about to *pop* from his head, pondered deeply, sighed, and said nothing. And so we laughed and sang and played and whiskied and soda-watered through the day. And fast the old *Northerner* rolled on. And at night the Captain gave us a grand game supper in his room, at which games we played not, but went at it in sober earnest; and then there were more songs (the same ones, though, and the same stories too, over again), and some speechifying, and much fun, until at eight bells we separated, some shouting, some laughing, some crying (but not with sorrow), but all extremely happy, and so we turned in. But before I sought stateroom A that night, I executed a small scheme, for insuring undisturbed repose, which I had revolved in my mind during the day, and which met with the most brilliant success, as you shall hear.

You remember the two snobs that every night, in the pursuit of exercise under difficulties, walk up and down on the deck, arm in arm, right over your stateroom. You remember how, when just as you are getting into your first doze, they commence, tramp! tramp! tramp! right over your head; then you "hear them fainter, fainter still;" you listen in horrible dread of their return, nourishing the while a feeble-minded hope that they may have gone below — when, horror! here they come, louder, louder, till tramp! tramp! tramp! they go over your head again, and with rage in your heart, at the conviction that sleep is impossible, you sit up in bed and despairingly light an unnecessary segar. They were on board the *Northerner,* and the night before had aroused my indignation to that strong pitch that I had determined on their downfall. So, before retiring, I proceeded to the upper deck, and there did I quietly attach a small cord to the stanchions which, stretching across about six inches from the planking, formed what in maritime matters is known as a "booby trap." This done, I repaired to my room, turned in, and calmly awaited the result. In ten minutes they came; I heard them laughing together as they mounted the ladder. Then commenced the exercise, louder,

louder, tramp! tramp! — thump! (a double-barreled thump) down they came together, "Oh, what a fall was there, my countrymen!" Two deep groans were elicited, and then followed what, if published, would make two closely printed royal octavo pages of profanity. I heard them d—n the soul of the man that did it. It was my soul that they alluded to, but I cared not, I lay there chuckling; "they called, but I answered not again," and when at length they limped away, their loud profanity subdued to a blasphemous growl, I turned over in a sweet frame of mind, and, falling instantaneously asleep, dreamed a dream, a happy dream of "home and thee" — Susan Ann Jane!

Ludwig Bemelmans
A Young Widow 1957

THE outstanding figure on that trip was a young widow. She was dressed in long, glamour-girl blond hair and black satin. I think she rubbed herself with a lotion every morning, and then pasted her clothes on her body; there wasn't a wrinkle in them. A doctor could have examined her as she was. Her arms were weighed down with bracelets, all of them genuine, and of course she had a silver fox jacket. An icebox full of orchids helped her bear up throughout the voyage. She appeared with fresh flowers at every meal, and she had with her a sad pale little girl, who was not allowed to play with other children. She wore a little mink coat on deck — the only junior mink I have ever seen.

The way the young widow managed her entrances into the dining-room reminded me of Easter at the Music Hall. She waited until the orchestra played Ravel's *Bolero* and then she came, surrounded by expensive vapors, heavy-lidded, the play of every muscle visible as a python's. At the first landing of the long stairs she bent down, while everyone held their breath, until she succeeded in picking up the train of her dress. Then a faultless ten inches of calf and ankle came into view and, with industrious little steps, she climbed down the rest of the stairs to the restaurant. Once seated, she smeared caviar on pieces of toast and garnished them with whites of eggs until they looked like the cards one sends to the bereaved; with this she drank champagne and looked out over the ocean. The sad little girl said nothing the whole day long.

The last night on board, the widow fell out of her role. A beautiful, exquisitely modeled, long, slim, gartered leg came dangling down from a high-held knee, out of black satin and lingerie. She danced like Jane Avril and let out a wild cowboy "Whoopee," blowing kisses to everyone.

Petroleum V. Nasby
Dear Mother 1882

AMONG the passengers was a young man from Oshkosh, Wisconsin, named Tibbitts. He was an excellent young man, of his kind, and he very soon acquired the reputation, which he deserved, of being the very best poker player on the ship. He was uneasy till a game was organized in the morning, and he growled ferociously when the lights were turned down at twelve at night. He was impatient with slow players, because, as he said, all the time they wasted was so much loss to him. He could drink more Scotch whisky than any one on the ship, and he was the pet of the entire crew, for his hand was always in his pocket. He ruined the rest of the passengers by his reckless liberality. His father was a rich Wisconsin farmer, and this was his first experience in travel.

What time he could spare from poker and his meals, was devoted to writing a letter to his mother, for whom the scapegrace did seem to have a great deal of respect and a very considerable amount of love. His letter was finished the day before we made Queenstown, so that he could mail it from there. He read it to me. The sentences in parenthesis were his comments: —

ON BOARD THE CITY OF RICHMOND,
NEAR QUEENSTOWN, May 23, 1881.

DEAR MOTHER: — While there is everything to interest one from the interior in a sea voyage, I confess that I have not enjoyed the passage at all. I have no heart for it for my mind is perpetually on you and my home in the far West. (*You see it will please the old lady to know I am thinking of her all the time. Didn't I scoop in that jack pot nicely last evening? Hadn't a thing in my hand, and Filkins actually opened it with three deuces.*) The ship is one of the strongest and best on the ocean, and is commanded and manned by the best sailors on the sea. The passengers are all good, serious people, with perhaps one exception. There is one young man from New York of dissolute habits, who has a bottle of whisky in his room, and who actually tried to tempt me to play cards with him. But he is known and avoided by the entire company.

We have regular services in the grand saloon, every morning, and occasional meetings for vocal exercises and conversation at other hours. I have just come from one, at which—

"You are not going to send this infernal aggregation of lies to your mother, are you?" I asked.

"Why not? She don't know any better, and it will make her feel good. I have my opinion of a man who won't give his old mother a pleasure when he can just as well as not. I will, you bet!"

"But such atrocious lies!"

"I'll chance that. I can stand lies of that kind when they are told in so good a cause. I love my mother, I do. Let's see, where was I? Oh yes."

I have just come from one at which the discussion was mostly on the progress of missions in the Far West. *(The old lady is Treasurer of a society for the conversion of the Apaches, or some other tribe.)* Just now the sailors are heaving a log, which they do to ascertain the speed the ship is making. Mr. Inman, the owner of this ship, is a very wealthy man, and he has everything of the best. He furnishes his vessel with nothing but black walnut logs to heave, and never uses profane language to his crew. On other ships the men who go aloft are compelled to climb tarred rope ladders, but Captain Leitch has passenger elevators rigged to the masts, such as you saw in the Palmer House in Chicago, in which they sit comfortably and are hoisted up by a steam engine.

"Great heavens! You are not surely going to send that?"

"Why not? What is an old lady in silver spectacles on a farm thirty miles from any water more than a well, going to know about a steamer? I must write her something, for she persuaded the old gentleman to let me take the trip. I ain't ungrateful, I ain't. I'll give her one good letter, anyhow. Why, by the way you talk, I should suppose you never had a mother, and if you had that you didn't know how to treat her. I hate a man who don't love his mother and isn't willing to sacrifice himself for her. All I can do for her now is to write to her, and write such letters as will interest her, and the dear old girl is going to get them, if the paper and ink holds out, and they are going to be good ones, too."

I have got to be a good deal of a sailor, and if it were not for leaving you, which I couldn't do, I believe I should take one of these ships myself. I know all about starboard and port — port used to be larboard — and I can tell the stern from the bow. On a ship you don't say, "I will go down stairs," but you say, "I will go below." One would think that I had been born on the sea, and was a true child of the ocean.

Owing to my strictly temperate habits at home, and my absolute abstemiousness on the ship, I have escaped the horrors of sea sickness. As you taught me, true happiness can only be found in virtue. The wicked young man from New York has been sick half the time, as a young man who keeps a bottle in his room should be.

The nice woolen stockings you knit for me have been a great comfort, and all I regret is, I am afraid I have not enough of them to last me till I get home.

(The young villain had purchased in New York an assortment of the most picturesque hosiery procurable, which he was wearing with low cut shoes. The woolen stockings he gave to his room-steward.)

The tracts you put in my valise I have read over and over again, and have lent them since to the passengers who prefer serious reading to trashy novels and literature of that kind. What time I have had to spare for other reading, I have devoted to books of travel, so that I may see Europe intelligently.

"By the way," he stopped to say, "are the Argyle rooms in London actually closed, and is the Mabille in Paris as lively as it used to be? Great Caesar! won't I make it lively for them!"

In another day we shall land in Liverpool, and then I shall be only five hours from London. I long to reach London, for I do so desire to hear Spurgeon, and attend the Exeter Hall meetings, as you desired me. But as we shall reach London on Tuesday, I shall be compelled to wait till the following Sunday — five long days.

Please ma, have pa send me a draft at my address at London, at once. I find the expense of travel is much greater than I supposed, and I fear I shall not have enough.

Your affectionate son,   LEMUEL.

"There," said Lemuel, as he sealed the letter, "that is what I call a good letter. The old lady will read it over and over to herself, and then she will read it to all the neighbors. It will do her a heap of good. Bye-bye. The boys are waiting for me in the smoking-room."

And stopping at the bar to take a drink — the liberality of English measure was not too great for him — he was, a minute after, absorbed in the mysteries of poker, and was "raking-in" the money of the others at a lively rate.

And the letter went to the good old mother, and probably did her good. And she, doubtless, worried the old gentleman till he sent the graceless fellow a remittance. Boys can always be sure of their mothers — would that mothers could only be half as sure of their boys.

S. G. Bayne
An Array of Proofs 1909

I T is impossible for any large body of travelers to escape the man who by every device tries to impress his fellows with the idea that he is a Mungo Park on his travels, and so our harmless impostor had his "trunkage" plastered with labels from all parts of the world, sold to him by hotel porters, who deal in them. He wore the fez, of course, and sported a Montenegrin order on his lapel; he had Turkish slippers; he carried a Malacca cane; he wrapped himself in a Mohave blanket and he wore a Caracas carved gold ring on his four-in-hand scarf. But his crowning effort was in wearing the great traveling badge, the English fore-and-aft checked cap, with its ear flaps tied up over the crown, leaving the front and rear scoops exposed. Not all of the passengers carried this array of proofs, but many dabbled in them just a little bit. It doesn't do, however, when assuming this rôle to have had your hair cut in Rome, New York, or to have bought your "pants" in Paris, Texas, for if you are guilty in those matters you will give the impression of being a mammoth comique on his annual holiday.

Harriet Beecher Stowe
An Old Traveler 1854

WHEN the ship has been out about eight days, an evident bettering of spirits and condition obtains among the passengers. Many of the sick ones take heart, and appear again among the walks and ways of men; the ladies assemble in little knots, and talk of getting on shore. The more knowing ones, who have travelled before, embrace this opportunity to show their knowledge of life by telling the new hands all sorts of hobgoblin stores about the custom house officers and the difficulties of getting landed in England. It is a curious fact, that old travellers generally seem to take this particular delight in striking consternation into younger ones.

"You'll have all your daguerreotypes taken away," says one lady, who, in right of having crossed the ocean nine times, is entitled to speak *ex cathedra* on the subject.

"All our daguerreotypes!" shriek four or five at once. "Pray tell, what for?"

"They *will do it*," says the knowing lady, with an awful nod; "unless you hide them and all your books, they'll burn up — "

"Burn our books!" exclaim the circle. "O, dreadful! What do they do that for?"

"They're very particular always to burn up all your books. I knew a lady who had a dozen burned," says the wise one.

"Dear me! will they take our *dresses?*" says a young lady, with increasing alarm.

"No, but they'll pull every thing out, and tumble them well over, I can tell you."

"How horrid!"

An old lady, who has been very sick all the way, is revived by this appalling intelligence.

"I hope they won't tumble over my *caps!*" she exclaims.

"Yes, they will have every thing out on deck," says the lady, delighted with the increasing sensation. "I tell you you don't know these custom house officers."

"It's too bad!" "It's dreadful!" "How horrid!" exclaim all.

"I shall put my best things in my pocket," exclaims one. "They don't search our pockets, do they?"

"Well, no, not here; but I tell you they'll search your *pockets* at Antwerp and Brussels," says the lady.

Somebody catches the sound, and flies off into the state rooms with the intelligence that "the custom house officers are so dreadful — they rip open your trunks, pull out all your things, burn your books, take away your daguerreotypes, and even search your pockets;" and a row of groans is heard ascending from the row of state rooms, as all begin to revolve what they have in their trunks, and what they are to do in this emergency.

"Pray tell me," said I to a gentlemanly man, who had crossed four or five times, "is there really so much annoyance at the custom house?"

"Annoyance, ma'am? No, not the slightest."

"But do they really turn out the contents of the trunks, and take away people's daguerreotypes, and burn their books?"

"Nothing of the kind, ma'am. I apprehend no difficulty. I never had any. There are a few articles on which duty is charged. I have a case of cigars, for instance; I shall show them to the custom house officer, and pay the duty. If a person seems disposed to be fair, there is no difficulty. The examination of ladies' trunks is merely nominal; nothing is deranged."

Irvin S. Cobb
A Medley of Voices 1914

I MAY say that I had one touch of climate fever going over and a succession of touches coming back.

At such a time, the companionship of others palls on one. It is well then to retire to the privacy of one's stateroom and recline awhile. I did a good deal of reclining, coming back; I was not exactly happy while reclining, but I was happier than I would have been doing anything else. Besides, as I reclined there on my cosy bed, a medley of voices would often float in to me through the half-opened port and I could visualize the owners of those voices as they sat ranged in steamer chairs, along the deck. I quote:

"You, Raymund! You get down off that rail this minute." . . . "My dear, you just ought to go to mine! He never hesitates a minute about operating, and he has the loveliest manners in the operating room. Wait a minute — I'll write his address down for you. Yes, he is expensive, but very, very thorough." . . . "Stew'd, bring me nozher brand' 'n' sozza." . . . "Well, now Mr. — excuse me, I didn't catch your name? — oh yes, Mr. Blosser; well, Mr. Blosser, if that isn't the most curious thing! To think of us meeting away out here in the middle of the ocean and both of us knowing Maxie Hockstein in Grand Rapids. It only goes to show one thing — this certainly is a mighty small world." . . . "Raymund, did you hear what I said to you!"

"Do you really think it is becoming? Thank you for saying so. That's what my husband always says. He says that white hair with a youthful face is so attractive, and that's one reason why I've never touched it up. Touched-up hair is so artificial, don't you think?" . . . "Wasn't the Bay of Naples just perfectly swell — the water, you know, and the land and the sky and everything, so beautiful and everything?" . . . "You Raymund, come away from that lifeboat. Why don't you sit down there and behave yourself and have a nice time watching for whales?" . . . "No, ma'am, if you're askin' me I must say I didn't care so much for that art gallery stuff — jest a lot of pictures and statues and junk like that, so far as I noticed. In fact the whole thing — Yurupp itself — was considerable of a disappointment to me. I didn't run acros't a single Knights of Pythias Lodge the whole time and I was over there five months straight hand-runnin'." . . . "Really, I think it must be hereditary; it runs in our family. I had an aunt and her hair was snow-white at twenty-one and my grandmother was the same way." . . . "Oh yes, the suffering is something terrible. You've had it yourself in a mild form and of course you know. The last time they operated on me, I was on the table an hour and forty minutes — mind you, an hour and forty minutes by the clock — and for three days and nights they didn't know whether I would live another minute."

A crash of glass.

"Stew'd, I ashidently turn' over m' drink — bring me nozher brand' 'n' sozza." . . . "Just a minute, Mr. Blosser, I want to tell my husband about it — he'll be awful interested. Say, listen, Poppa, this gentleman here knows Maxie Hockstein out in Grand Rapids." . . . "Do you think so, really? A lot of people have said that very same thing to me. They come up to me and say 'I know you must be a Southerner because you have such a true Southern accent.' I suppose I must come by it naturally, for while I was born in New Jersey, my mother was a member of a very old Virginia family and we've always been very strong Southern sympathizers and I went to a finishing school in Baltimore and I was always being mistaken for a Southern girl." . . . "Well, I sure had enough of it to do me for one spell. I seen the whole shootin' match and I don't regret what it cost me, but, believe me, little old Keokuk is goin' to look purty good to me when I get back there. Why, them people don't know no more about makin' a cocktail than a rabbit." . . . "That's her standing yonder talking to the captain. Yes, that's what so many people say, but as a matter of fact, she's the youngest one of the two. I say, 'These are my daughters,' and then people say, 'You mean your sisters.' Still I married very young — at seventeen — and possibly that helps to explain it." . . . "Oh, is that a shark out yonder? Well, anyway, it's a porpoise, and a porpoise is a kind of shark, isn't it? When a porpoise grows up, it gets to be a shark — I read that somewhere. Ain't nature just wonderful?" . . . "Raymund Walter Pelham, if I have to speak to you again, young man, I'm going to take you to the stateroom and give you something you won't forget in a hurry." . . . "Stew'd, hellup me gellup."

Thus the lazy hours slip by and the spell of the sea takes hold on you and you lose count of the time and can barely muster up the energy to perform the regular noonday task of putting your watch back half an hour. A passenger remarks that this is Thursday and you wonder dimly what happened to Wednesday.

"I'm afraid you're misinformed – I'm not empowered to marry you."

❧Captain and Crew

❧*Of all the people one meets on a cruise, with the exception of new loves (up to six; beyond that they tend to blur), no one is more memorable than the captain. It is his table you long to sit at, his outfit you long to be able to wear, his power you long to command. On the captain, we have a piece of drama by the indubitable Frank Sullivan which gets very close to home, but first a poem by Phyllis McGinley, the only writer of light verse to win a Pulitzer Prize.*

Phyllis McGinley
Cruise Captain's Chantey 1937

Captain S —— is not only an experienced seaman, of the old tradition, but also a jovial master of ceremonies. — *Travel Folder.*

> *Oh, merry was a sailor's life when we went down to Rio,*
> > *But now we go a-cruising, it is merrier than that.*
> *For I can offer prizes for a ukulele trio*
> > *And often, after dinner, I can wear a paper hat.*

When I was a lad of two or three
  (Or maybe a little sooner),
I found the sea and I shipped at sea
  Aboard of a noble schooner,
And I was trained for a sailor brave,
  To chuckle at all disaster,
To tame the billow and dare the wave
  From the deck of a seven-master.
But cups will slip from the eagerest lip
  And life is a curious choosing,
So now I've an air-conditioned ship
  And take my passengers cruising.

For this I won me a braided coat
    And rose above my cronies,
That I might captain a cruising boat
    As master of ceremonies.
Heave ho, my lads, heave ho, heave ho,
    I'm master of ceremonies.

For this I followed the sea birds' tracks
    And learned the ways of ocean,
That restless ladies in cotton slacks
    Could chide me about the motion,
That I might jovially consort
    With gentlemen oddly mobile,
And pour them on at many a port
    Or pour them off at Cristobal.
For this I battled the bold monsoon
    And round the Horn made journey,
That I could dandle a toy balloon
    Or sponsor a contract tourney.
Then blow your worst, O furious gale,
    With impotent wrath and petty!
A tropical cruise can never fail
    If we have enough confetti.
Heave ho, my lads, heave nautically ho,
    We'll carry enough confetti.

Oh, merry was a sailor's life when stars inspired our courses,
    But now we go a-cruising, it is merrier than that.
For I can watch the races of the numbered wooden horses,
    And later, after dinner, I can wear a paper hat.

Frank Sullivan
Captain's Dinner *c1935*

WE are at the captain's table aboard the ferry *Grover A. Whalen* plying between South Ferry and Staten Island, shortly before arrival at Staten Island. Two passengers enter, Mrs. Shirley Levine and Mrs. Francis X. O'Hara.

MRS. LEVINE: How do you do? I don't believe I've had the pleasure of meeting you.

MRS. O'HARA: How do you do? I'm Mrs. O'Hara.

MRS. LEVINE: How do you do, Mrs. O'Hara, I'm Mrs. Levine.

MRS. O'HARA: How do you do, Mrs. Levine. To tell the truth, I haven't been much in evidence since we left South Ferry. I'm a rather poor sailor. I kept to my cabin pretty much. But of course the captain's dinner — one simply couldn't miss that, could one?

MRS. LEVINE: Aren't they fun? I simply adore them. And our captain. He's too divine for words.

MRS. O'HARA: I caught a brief glimpse of him as I came aboard and liked the cut of his jib, as they say, very much. But hasn't it been rather a swift crossing? It seems scarcely ten minutes since we left the Battery.

MRS. LEVINE: One doesn't notice time passing on a voyage to Staten Island. There are so many things to do . . . I wonder whom we've drawn as partners for the captain's dinner. I do hope I don't get that horrible Corporal Dinwiddie from Fort Jay. My dear, he's been trying to pinch me ever since we left South Ferry.

MRS. LEVINE: All men are beasts!

MRS. O'HARA: Well, I mean, at least I don't think such intimacies are quite justified, even allowing for the informality that is inevitable on a sea trip where one is thrown together so much.

MRS. O'HARA: Anyhow, not until one has passed Governor's Island . . . I seem to have drawn a Colonel D'Arcy Fingle.

MRS. LEVINE: Oh, lucky you! Colonel Fingle is terrible interesting. *Très distingué.*

MRS. O'HARA: *Vraiment? Commong?*

MRS. LEVINE: He spends all his time traveling between South Ferry and Staten Island.

MRS. O'HARA: In heaven's name, my dear, why?

MRS. LEVINE: To — forget.

MRS. O'HARA: How too utterly romantic. It's a woman, of course. When one hears that a man goes to Staten Island to forget, one always assumes that a woman is at the bottom of it.

MRS. LEVINE: As I understand it, he *thinks* it is a woman he is trying to forget, but is no longer quite sure. He has made 21,000 crossings, and since the 10,000th he has forgotten what it was he was trying to forget.

MRS. O'HARA: He sounds too divine. Whom have you drawn?

MRS. LEVINE: *(looking at her place card):* Ah, Signor Pastolozzi.

MRS. O'HARA: Pray, whom is he?

MRS. LEVINE: The ship's bootblack. Perfectly fascinating Latin type. Full of *élan vital.*

MRS. O'HARA: *Elan vital.* How splendid.

(Signor Arturo Pastolozzi enters.)

PASTOLOZZI: Shine? Shine 'em up? Shine?

MRS. LEVINE: How do you *do,* Signor Pastolozzi? Mrs. O'Hara, may I present Signor Pastolozzi?

MRS. O'HARA: Charmed, I'm sure.

PASTOLOZZI: Shine? Shine 'em up, Mrs. O'Hara?

MRS. LEVINE: *(tapping Pastolozzi with her fan):* Ah, you men! Must you always be talking of business? Come now, Signor, forget your shines and your shoe polish for the nonce and be a nice boy. Sit down. You are placed next me at dinner. I shall expect you to be very, very witty.

PASTOLOZZI: Shine? Shine 'em up?

(Captain Delehanty of the Grover A. Whalen *and Colonel D'Arcy Fingle enter).*

CAPTAIN: Good evening all, and you are welcome to *Grover A. Whalen.* I assume everyone knows everyone else. I pride myself that on my boat people do not remain strangers long. I like to think of my passengers as just one big happy family.

(At this point a man enters and walks through the dining saloon, crying in a bitter voice, "I do not want to go to Staten Island!" He exits.)

PASTOLOZZI: Shine?

MRS. LEVINE: Captain Delehanty, I insist you do something about this naughty boy. He will talk of nothing but business, business, business.

CAPTAIN: Relax, Pastolozzi. All work and no play, you know. And remember, you can't take your money with you when you go.

COL. FINGLE *(to Mrs. Levine):* Is this your first crossing, may I ask?

MRS. LEVINE: Oh, dear, no. I make the trip practically every week, to see my sister in Stapleton. I do think there is nothing like a trip down the bay to give one the feeling of getting away from it all. I love the life aboard a ferry. The moment the boat leaves the Battery, I begin to feel relaxed and rested. One has that blessed sense of being far from the reach of the maddening telephone *(a telephone rings somewhere)* and equally far from that vile distracting riveting. *(Distant riveting is heard.)*

COL. FINGLE: I agree with you utterly. I think everyone should go to Staten Island at least once every week.

(That man walks across the stage again, bellowing "I do not want to go to Staten Island, ever.")

MRS. O'HARA: Pray, whom is that interesting-looking young man?

COL. FINGLE: There's quite a story about him. He doesn't want to go to Staten Island. But he has to.

MRS. LEVINE: How interesting. Why?

COL. FINGLE: He was a dick on the Manhattan police force. He made the mistake of pinching a politician in a raid on a — a —

(Colonel Fingle blushes furiously, and is embarrassed.)

MRS. O'HARA: Please go on, Colonel. Please don't mind us.

COL. FINGLE: Oh, thank you, dear lady. A raid on a house of — ill fame.

MRS. LEVINE: A house of ill fame. How too perfectly romantic.

COL. FINGLE: How nice of you to say so, ma'am. So now he has to pound the pavements in Staten Island. He hates the thought.

CAPTAIN: Well, I guess the time has come, as the walrus said, for me to inflict my usual speech on you good folks . . .

(Cries of "He's going to speak" and "Oh, good!" and "Quiet there, the Captain's going to speak.")

CAPTAIN: I haven't any idea why a speech should be expected of the Captain on an occasion like this, and I certainly am no speech-maker . . .

(Cries of "Oh, yes you are" and "You are, too" and "Don't be so modest.")

CAPTAIN: However, the sooner I get it over with, the sooner you folks can go ahead and enjoy yourselves. So — uh — ladies and gentlemen — if I may call you ladies and gentlemen . . .

(Cries of "Isn't that delicious?" and "Isn't he a card?" and "Don't you love his sense of humor?")

CAPTAIN: I am only going to say a few words . . .

(There is a violent jarring and jolting. Suggs, a mate, hurries in.)

CAPTAIN *(apprehensively)*: Yes? What is it?

SUGGS: Sir, a grapefruit rind caught in the propeller. You'd better come.

(Panicked murmurings of "Good God, a grapefruit rind in the propeller!" and "Did you hear that? We have been struck by a grapefruit!")

CAPTAIN: Ladies and gentlemen, I beg of you — please remain calm. There is absolutely no cause for alarm. Please carry on, Von Bismarck.

VON BISMARCK *(the ship's accordion player)*: Here, sir.

CAPTAIN: Von Bismarck, play.

(Von Bismarck plays "Columbia, the gem of the Ocean." Everyone is calmed. Von Bismarck passes the hat.)

PASTOLOZZI: Shine? Anybody want a shine?

MRS. LEVINE: I have every confidence in Captain Delehanty. He is a seasoned navigator and has dealt with greater crises than grapefruit rinds.

MRS. O'HARA: Colonel Fingle, I understand that you spend all your time traveling on ferryboats — to forget.

COL. FINGLE: Dear lady, one can never forget the past. One only forgets the future.

MRS. O'HARA: How true that is.

COL. FINGLE: And no matter what ferry one is on, one can never escape from one's memories.

MRS. O'HARA: I — understand. Was she — beautiful?

COL. FINGLE: I don't know. I forget.

MRS. O'HARA: I understand. I too have loved — and suffered.

COL. FINGLE: Life, Mrs. O'Hara, is just one long trip on a ferryboat.

MRS. O'HARA: And we the passengers. How true.

(Captain Delehanty returns.)

CAPTAIN: Forgive me. So sorry to have interrupted the revelry.

MRS. LEVINE: You poor dear, I certainly do not envy a ferry boat captain his job.

CAPTAIN: Huh, I'm having a comparatively easy time of it this trip. I've seen trips when I've had to stay on the bridge fifteen, twenty minutes steady.

MRS. LEVINE: How *can* you stand it?

CAPTAIN: Well, I knew a sailor's life was no bed of roses when I started.

MRS. LEVINE: You know, I once crossed on the Fort Lee ferry when the outboard motorboats were having their race from Albany. The river was simply crammed with them and do you know our captain never left the bridge for an instant during that trip?

CAPTAIN: Of course, the Hudson is a mere brook compared with the Bay.

MRS. LEVINE: I was taking my daughter, Eloise, to Palisade Park.

MRS. O'HARA: How nice for her.

MRS. LEVINE: I thought she ought to "do" Palisade before she came out. A young girl should have some background, you know, and one meets such interesting people at Palisade. Eloise picked up some very eligible young sailors while we were there.

CAPTAIN: Well, I guess I'll make another, what do you call it, "stab" at that confounded speech . . . Ladies and gentlemen; Friends, Romans and Countrymen . . .

(Cries of "Friends, Romans and Countrymen — isn't he killing!")

CAPTAIN: I am only going to say a few words . . .

(There is another jolt and everybody is knocked off his seat.)

SUGGS: Sir.

CAPTAIN: *Now* what is it?

SUGGS: Sir, we've hit a garbage scow.

(Cries of "Good God, a garbage scow!" and "Did you hear that, we've hit a garbage scow.")

CAPTAIN: Every man to his post. Ladies and gentlemen, I assure you there is no cause for alarm. Absolutely no danger. Von Bismarck.

VON BISMARCK: Yes, sir.

CAPTAIN: Play.

(Von Bismarck plays "Rule Britannia" and calms everyone. Passes the hat.)

MRS. O'HARA: I have every confidence in Captain Delehanty. I am sure he will bring us safely to Staten Island.

(The man walks across the stage, moaning, "I don't want to go to Staten Island.")

MRS. O'HARA: I am thinking of making the Grand Tour next month. Mr. O'Hara has been running an elevator in the Equitable Building for fifteen years now without a vacation, and I think he ought to go somewhere horizontally for a change. I've sent for booklets. I think we'll start with the trip to Hoboken.

COL. FINGLE: My dear Mrs. O'Hara, I strongly urge you not to go to Hoboken during the glue season.

MRS. O'HARA: I am told the seasonal winds will be blowing toward Bayonne by the time we start. Then of course we'd do the Weehawken trip, the Fort Lee and Dyckman Street, and then we plan to cross the International Date Line to the East River and wind up with the trip on the Astoria ferry, which they say is divine.

(That man who didn't want to go to Staten Island now sticks his head in the door and says, "Confidentially, between you and I, I wouldn't want to go to Astoria, either.")

MRS. LEVINE: My dear, let me tell you the Grand Tour is all very well, but you get awfully sick of it. Levine and I did it last summer and the poor man was so ferry-sore by the time we got to Astoria, and so homesick for the Bronx, that we simply had to call everything off, charter a scow and row him up the Harlem to 167th street. Ah, here's Captain Delehanty back. Is everything all right, Captain?

CAPTAIN: Everything is under control, ma'am. One of those confounded garbage scows from the upper East Side got messy. Just because they carry old discarded bits of caviar and truffles they seem to think they are lords and masters of the sea.

MRS. O'HARA: Where are we now, Captain? Shall we reach Staten Island on schedule?

CAPTAIN: Oh, I think so. We passed through a shoal of grapefruit off Governor's Island that slowed us up a bit, but I think we'll make up the lost time, unless we run into the Bay Ridge mistral, which is due any time now. Well, you know the old saying, if at first you don't succeed —

(Cries of "Isn't he a caution?" and "Oh, I wish I could think of things like that to say.")

CAPTAIN: So here goes for another try at that speech. Ladies and gentlemen, I am only going to say a few words . . .

(There is a crash.)

CAPTAIN: Oh, dear, sometimes it seems as if a person never got a moment's peace aboard this boat. You know, sometimes I get so nervous I just feel like jumping out of my skin.

(Suggs, the mate, enters.)

CAPTAIN: What is it NOW, you . . . !

SUGGS: Staten Island. All out.

᳴*And then there's the crew, all those people who have helped you through so much. Travel writers, even humorists, find it hard to say nasty things about stewards and stewardesses, except that they're too good to be true. But sailors are another thing altogether.*

Stephen Longstreet
Stewards 1941

THE stewards are a class by themselves. They — with the pursers — are people too good for the diplomatic service, deep students of human nature. Cynics, hardened followers of Plato and Jesse James.

Years afloat in the tourist trade has hardened their skins and given them masks of smooth sagacity for faces. They can get you anything, allow anything, fix anything and hide anything. As I watch them in their spotless white, gliding along halls and spinning past doors and bowing to the right people, I wonder how many bodies they have cut apart with hack saws and shoved out of portholes, how many pounds of dope they have smuggled in, what honest Boston matron they have sold to the white slave hell of South America (where the follower of Emerson and Lowell now dances the nude can-can with a rose in her Back Bay teeth). Perhaps the last suggestion is wishful thinking. The Boston accent is beginning to chafe me. It treats all other accents like moral leprosy.

Charles Dickens
A Piously Fraudulent
Stewardess 1842

HAVING settled this point to the perfect satisfaction of all parties, concerned and unconcerned, we sat down round the fire in the ladies' cabin — just to try the effect. It was rather dark, certainly; but somebody said, "Of course it would be light at sea," a proposition to which we all assented, echoing "of course, of course;" though it would be exceedingly difficult to say why we thought so. I remember, too, when we had discovered and exhausted another topic of consolation in the circumstance of this ladies' cabin adjoining our state-room, and the consequently immense feasibility of sitting there at all times and seasons, and had fallen into a momentary silence, leaning our faces on our hands and looking at the fire, one of our party said, with the solemn air of a man who had made a discovery, "What a relish mulled claret will have down here!" which appeared to strike us all most forcibly, as though there were something spicy and high-flavoured in cabins which essentially improved that composition and rendered it quite incapable of perfection anywhere else.

There was a stewardess, too, actively engaged in producing clean sheets and tablecloths from the very entrails of the sofas, and from unexpected lockers, of such artful mechanism that it made one's head ache to see them opened one after another, and rendered it quite a distracting circumstance to follow her proceedings, and to find that every nook and corner and individual piece of furniture was something else besides what it pretended to be, and was a mere trap and deception and place of secret stowage, whose ostensible purpose was its least useful one.

God bless the stewardess for her piously fraudulent account of January voyages! God bless her for her clear recollection of the companion passage of last year, when nobody was ill, and everybody danced from morning to night, and it was "a run" of twelve days, and a piece of the purest frolic, and delight, and jollity! All happiness be with her for her bright face and her pleasant Scotch tongue, which had sounds of old Home in it for my fellow-traveller; and for her predictions of fair winds and fine weather (all wrong, or I shouldn't be half so fond of her); and for the ten thousand small fragments of genuine womanly tact, by which, without piecing them elaborately together, and patching them up into shape and form and case and pointed application, she nevertheless did plainly show that all young mothers on one side of the Atlantic were near and close at hand to their little children left upon the other; and that what seemed to the uninitiated a serious journey was, to those who were in the secret, a mere frolic, to be sung about and whistled at! Light be her heart, and gay her merry eyes, for years!

William Dean Howells
His Part of the Joke 1899

I N the prompt monotony the time was already passing swiftly. The deck-steward seemed hardly to have been round with tea and bouillon, and he had not yet gathered up all the empty cups, when the horn for lunch sounded. It was the youngest of the table-stewards who gave the summons to meals; and wherever the pretty boy appeared with his bugle, funny passengers gathered round him to make him laugh, and stop him from winding it. His part of the joke was to fulfil his duty with gravity, and only to give way to a smile of triumph as he walked off.

Petroleum V. Nasby
Not What He Used to Be 1882

A VOYAGE at sea is not what it was when first I sailed from — but no, I have never been abroad before, and have not, therefore, the privilege of lying about travel. That will come in time, and doubtless I shall use it as others do. But I was going to say that sailing is not what it was, as I understand it to have been. The ship of to-day is nothing more or less than a floating hotel, with some few of the conveniences omitted, and a great many conveniences that hotels on shore have not. You have your luxurious barber-shop, you have a gorgeous bar, you have hot and cold water in your room, and a table as good as the best in New York. You eat, drink, and sleep just as well, if not better, than on shore.

The sailor is no more what he used to be than the ship is. I have seen any number of sailors, and know all about them. The tight young fellow in blue jacket and shiny tarpaulin, and equally shiny belt, and white trousers, the latter enormously wide at the bottom, which trousers he was always hitching up with a very peculiar movement of the body, standing first upon one leg and then upon the other; the sailor who could fight three pirates at once and kill them all, finishing the last one by disabling his starboard eye with a chew of tobacco thrown with terrible precision; who, if an English sailor, was always a match for three Frenchmen, if an American a match for three Englishmen, and no matter of what nationality, was always ready to d—n the eyes of the man he did not like, and protect prepossessing females and oppressed children even at the risk of being hung at the yard-arm by a court-martial — this kind of a sailor is gone, and I fear forever. I know I have given a proper description of him, for I have seen hundreds of them — at the theater.

In his stead is an unpoetic being, clad in all sorts of unpoetic clothing, and no two of them alike. There is a faint effort at uniformity in their caps, which have sometimes the name of their ship on them, but even that not always. In fair weather he is in appearance very like a hod carrier, and in foul weather a New York drayman. He doesn't d—n anybody's eyes, and he doesn't sing out "Belay there," or "Avast, you lubber," or indulge in any other nautical expressions. He uses just about the language that people on shore do, and is as dull and uninteresting a person as one would wish not to meet.

The traditional jack tar, of whom the Dibden of the last century sang, only remains in "Pinafore" opera, and can only be seen when the nautical pieces of the thirty years ago are revived. If such sailors ever existed, off the stage, they are as extinct a race as the icthyosaurus. Steam has knocked the poetry out of navigation, as it has out of everything else — that is, that kind of poetry. It will doubtless have a poetry of its own, when it gets older, but it is too new yet.

There is no holystoning the decks. On the contrary the decks are washed with hose, and scrubbed afterward by a patent appliance, which has nothing of the old time about it. The lifting is done by steam, and in fact every blessed thing about the ship is done by machinery. There is neither a ship nor a sailor any more. There are floating hotels, and help. The last remaining show for a ship is the masts and sails they all have, and they seem to be more for ornament than use.

Mark Twain
Showing Her the Ropes 1897

SEPT. 5. Closing in on the equator this noon. A sailor explained to a young girl that the ship's speed is poor because we are climbing up the bulge toward the center of the globe; but that when we should once get over, at the equator, and start down-hill, we should fly.

When she asked him the other day what the foreyard was, he said it was the front yard, the open area in the front end of the ship. That man has a good deal of learning stored up, and the girl is likely to get it all.

Sailor's Consolation

One night came on a hurricane,
  The sea was mountains rolling,
When Barney Buntline turned his quid,
  And said to Billy Bowline:
"A strong nor'wester's blowing, Bill.
  Hark! Don't you hear it roar now?
Lord help them! How I pities all
  Unlucky folks on shore now.

"Foolhardy chaps that live in towns;
  What dangers they are all in,
And now lie shaking in their beds
  For fear the roof should fall in.
Poor creatures, how they envy us
  And wishes, I've a notion,
For our good luck in such a storm
  To be upon the ocean.

"And often, Bill, I have been told
  How folks are killed, and undone,
By overturns of carriages,
  By fogs and fires in London.
We know what risks all landsmen run,
  From noblemen to tailors,
Then, Bill, let us thank Providence
  That you and me are sailors."
      — *William Pitt, 19th cent.*

A CHOIR OF 300 MIXED VOICES FROM THE SOUTH BETHLEHEM TONKUNST AND LIEDERKRANZ SOCIETY BURST INTO CHORUS—AND THE WHALE WAS SLOWLY LIFTED OUT OF THE OCEAN.

THE SEA AROUND YOU

❧The Sea and Its Wildlife

❧*Though you may tire of looking out over its blank horizons or sicken at the thought of its waves, it is to the sea that all cruiseship passengers should pay homage. The heavens might be fine for astronauts, but the closest we'll ever get to the weightlessness of the great vacuum up there is low-altitude turbulence. Compared to the endless billboards of the roadways and the uncountable poles of the railways, the blankness of the sea's horizons comes to seem welcome and soothing. And when they fill, with sunrises and sunsets and far-off storms, there's no better spectacle, even around the pool.*

But the rules of the humorists' union forbid its members to be the slightest bit romantic. Forty days without a sunset is something they can write about, but not the sunset of the forty-first. They can write about the effect on us of the powerful ocean, but only in contrast to the effect on us of its powerful motion. Four lines is enough for a humorist of Anonymous's skills to take on over 2/3 of the earth's surface.

> The Sea
> Behold the wonders of the mighty deep,
> Where crabs and lobsters learn to creep,
> And little fishes learn to swim,
> And clumsy sailors tumble in.

The others need a little more space. You should come away from their examination appreciating (or, possibly, depreciating) the sea more than you ever did before.

Lewis Carroll
A Sea Dirge 1869

There are certain things — a spider, a ghost,
   The income-tax, gout, an umbrella for three —
That I hate, but the thing that I hate the most
   Is a thing they call the SEA.

Pour some cold water over the floor —
   Ugly I'm sure you'll allow it to be:
Suppose it extended a mile or more,
   That's very like the SEA.

Beat a dog till it howls outright —
   Cruel, but all very well for a spree:
Suppose that one did so day and night,
   That would be like the SEA.

I had a vision of nursery-maids;
   Tens of thousands passed by me —
All leading children with wooden spades,
   And this was by the SEA.

Who invented those spades of wood?
   Who was it cut them out of the tree?
None, I think, but an idiot could —
   Or one that loved the SEA.

It is pleasant and dreamy, no doubt, to float
   With 'thoughts as boundless, and souls as free';
But suppose you are very unwell in a boat,
   How do you like the SEA?

There is an insect that people avoid
   (Whence is derived the verb 'to flee')
Where have you been by it most annoyed?
   In lodgings by the SEA.

If you like coffee with sand for dregs,
   A decided hint of salt in your tea,
And a fishy taste in the very eggs —
   By all means choose the SEA.

And if, with these dainties to drink and eat,
   You prefer not a vestige of grass or tree,
And a chronic state of wet in your feet,
   Then — I recommend the SEA.

For *I* have friends who dwell by the coast,
    Pleasant friends they are to me!
It is when I'm with them I wonder most
    That anyone likes the SEA.

They take me a walk: though tired and stiff,
    To climb the heights I madly agree:
And, after a tumble or so from the cliff,
    They kindly suggest the SEA.

I try the rocks, and I think it cool
    That they laugh with such an excess of glee,
As I heavily slip into every pool
    That skirts the cold, cold SEA.

Finley Peter Dunne
That Anny Man Cud Cross *1910*

"AN' there ye ar-re. A boat's a boat aven whin it looks like a hotel. But it's wondherful annyhow. Whin ye come to think iv it 'tis wondherful that anny man cud cross th' Atlantic in annything. Th' Atlantic Ocean is a fine body iv wather, but it's a body iv wather just th' same. It wasn't intinded to be thravelled on. Ye cud put ye'er foot through it annywhere. It's sloppy goin' at best. Th' on'y time a human being can float in it is afther he's dead. A man throws a horse-shoe into it an' th' horseshoe sinks. This makes him cross an' he builds a boat iv th' same mateeryal as a millyon horseshoes, loads it up with machinery, pushes it out on th' billows an' goes larkin' acrost thim as aisy as ye plaze. If he didn't go over on a large steel skyscraper he'd take a dure off its hinges an' go on that.

"All ye have to do is to tell him there's land on th' other side iv th' ragin' flood an' he'll say: 'All right, I'll take a look at it.' Ye talk about th' majesty iv th' ocean but what about th' majesty iv this here little sixty-eight be eighteen inches bump iv self-reliance that treats it like th' dirt undher his feet? It's a wondher to me that th' ocean don't get tired iv growlin' an' roarin' at th' race iv men. They don't pay anny heed to it's hollering. Whin it behaves itsilf they praise it as though it was a good dog. 'How lovely our ocean looks undher our moon.' Whin it rises in its wrath they show their contimpt f'r it be bein' sea-sick into it. But no matther how it behaves they niver quit usin' its face f'r a right iv way. They'll niver subjoo it but it niver bates thim. There niver was a time in th' history iv little man's sthruggle with th' vasty deep that he didn't deserve a decision on points."

"Well, it's all very well, but f'r me th' dhry land," said Mr. Hennessy. "Will ye iver cross th' ocean again?"

"Not," said Mr. Dooley, "till they asphalt it an' run th' boats on throlleys."

Eva Ogden
The Sea

She was rich, and of high degree;
A poor and unknown artist he.
"Paint me," she said, "a view of the sea."

So he painted the sea as it looked the day
That Aphrodite arose from its spray;
And it broke, as she gazed on its face the while,
Into its countless-dimpled smile.
"What a pokey, stupid picture!" said she;
"I don't believe he can paint the sea!"

Then he painted a raging, tossing sea,
Storming, with fierce and sudden shock,
Wild cries, and writhing tongues of foam,
A towering, mighty fastness-rock.
In its sides, above those leaping crests,
The thronging sea-birds built their nests.
"What a disagreeable daub!" said she;
"Why, it isn't anything like the sea!"

Then he painted a stretch of hot, brown sand,
With a big hotel on either hand
And a handsome pavilion for the band —
Not a sign of the water to be seen
Except one faint little streak of green.
"What a perfectly exquisite picture!" said she;
It's the very image of the sea!"

Phyllis McGinley
The Sea Chantey Around Us 1954

How vast, how clean
  The ageless ocean!
Whether serene
  Or in commotion,
Haunted by gull
  Or dolphin set,
How beautiful,
  How wild and wet!

Though rich and rare
  Its fauna and flora,
No evening's there
  And no aurora;
Instead, I think,
  A great supply
Of pearls and ink-
  Y octopi.

From pole to pole
  What whales take cover in,
The moon its sole
  Capricious sovereign,
Speaking in thunders
  Through its sleep,
Ah, rife with wonders
  Is the deep!

The waters tell it,
The billows shout it.
And I'm fed to the teeth with books about it.

ఴ*The sea is, of course, much more than a few billion gallons of water
with a pinch of salt. It is also what swims under, and jumps over, its
surface, from the tiniest plankton to the greatest of the great whales.
In fact, almost as interesting as the people on a cruise — some, in fact
many, would say more — are the animals one encounters in the water,
in the air, on the ship, and, in the instance of a flying fish that lands
pooped on the deck, all three. Animals seem to attract the poet more
than the prose writer, except, of course, for Mark Twain.*

Leigh Hunt
To a Fish

You strange, astonished-looking, angle-faced,
 Dreary-mouthed, gaping wretches of the sea,
 Gulping salt-water everlastingly,
Cold-blooded, though with red your blood be graced,
And mute, though dwellers in the roaring waste;
 And you, all shapes beside, that fishy be, —
 Some round, some flat, some long, all devilry,
Legless, unloving, infamously chaste; —

O scaly, slippery, wet, swift, staring wights,
 What is't ye do? What life lead? eh, dull goggles?
How do ye vary your vile days and nights?
 How pass your Sundays? Are ye still but joggles
In ceaseless wash! Still nought but gapes, and bites,
 And drinks, and stares, diversified with boggles?

Leigh Hunt
A Fish Answers

Amazing monster! that, for aught I know,
 With the first sight of thee didst make our race
 For ever stare! O flat and shocking face,
Grimly divided from the breast below!
Thou that on dry land horribly dost go
 With a split body and most ridiculous pace,
 Prong after prong, disgracer of all grace,
Long-useless-finned, haired, upright, unwet, slow!
O breather of unbreathable, sword-sharp air,
 How canst exist? How bear thyself, thou dry
And dreary sloth? What particle canst share
 Of the only blessed life, the watery?
I sometimes see of ye an actual *pair*
 Go by! linked fin by fin! most odiously.

Mark Twain
The Kitten of the Sea *1897*

SEPT. 15 — *Night.* Close to Australia now. Sydney 50 miles distant.

That note recalls an experience. The passengers were sent for, to come up in the bow and see a fine sight. It was very dark. One could not follow with the eye the surface of the sea more than fifty yards in any direction — it dimmed away and became lost to sight at about that distance from us. But if you patiently gazed into the darkness a little while, there was a sure reward for you. Presently, a quarter of a mile away you would see a blinding splash or explosion of light on the water — a flash so sudden and so astonishingly brilliant that it would make you catch your breath; then that blotch of light would instantly extend itself and take the corkscrew shape and imposing length of the fabled sea-serpent, with every curve of its body and the "break" spreading away from its head, and the wake following behind its tail clothed in a fierce splendor of living fire. And my, but it was coming at a lightning gait! Almost before you could think, this monster of light, fifty feet long, would go flaming and storming by, and suddenly disappear. And out in the distance whence he came you would see another flash; and another and another and another, and see them turn into sea-serpents on the instant; and once sixteen flashed up at the same time and came tearing toward us, a swarm of wiggling curves, a moving conflagration, a vision of bewildering beauty, a spectacle of fire and energy whose equal the most of those people will not see again until after they are dead.

It was porpoises — porpoises aglow with phosphorescent light. They presently collected in a wild and magnificent jumble under the bows, and there they played for an hour, leaping and frolicking and carrying on, turning summersaults in front of the stem or across it and never getting hit, never making a miscalculation, though the stem missed them only about an inch, as a rule. They were porpoises of the ordinary length — eight or ten feet — but every twist of their bodies sent a long procession of united and glowing curves astern. That fiery jumble was an enchanting thing to look at, and we stayed out the performance; one cannot have such a show as that twice in a lifetime. The porpoise is the kitten of the sea; he never has a serious thought, he cares for nothing but fun and play. But I think I never saw him at his winsomest until that night. It was near a center of civilization, and he could have been drinking.

Wallace Irwin
The Rhyme of the
Chivalrous Shark 1904

Most chivalrous fish of the ocean,
　　To ladies forbearing and mild,
Though his record be dark, is the man-eating shark
　　Who will eat neither woman nor child.

He dines upon seamen and skippers,
　　And tourists his hunger assuage,
And a fresh cabin boy will inspire him with joy
　　If he's past the maturity age.

A doctor, a lawyer, a preacher,
　　He'll gobble one any fine day,
But the ladies, God bless 'em, he'll only address 'em
　　Politely and go on his way.

I can readily cite you an instance
　　Where a lovely young lady of Breem,
Who was tender and sweet and delicious to eat,
　　Fell into the bay with a scream.

She struggled and flounced in the water
　　And signaled in vain for her bark,
And she'd surely been drowned if she hadn't been found
　　By a chivalrous man-eating shark.

He bowed in a manner most polished,
　　Thus soothing her impulses wild;
"Don't be frightened," he said, "I've been properly bred
　　And will eat neither woman nor child."

Then he proffered his fin and she took it —
　　Such a gallantry none can dispute —
While the passengers cheered as the vessel they neared
　　And a broadside was fired in salute.

And they soon stood alongside the vessel,
　　When a life-saving dingey was lowered
With the pick of the crew, and her relatives, too,
　　And the mate and the skipper aboard.

So they took her aboard in a jiffy,
　　And the shark stood attention the while,

Then he raised on his flipper and ate up the skipper
   And went on his way with a smile.

And this shows that the prince of the ocean,
   To ladies forbearing and mild,
Though his record be dark, is the man-eating shark
   Who will eat neither woman nor child.

Jarvis Keiley
The Song of a Jellyfish

As the waves slip over my cuticle sleek
   They tickle my soul with glee,
And I shake with a visceral, saccharine joy
   In the place where my ribs should be.
      For I'm simply a lump of limpid lard,
         With a gluey sort of a wish
      To pass my time in the oozing slime —
         In the home of the jellyfish.

But I'm happy in having no bones to break
   In my unctuous, waving form,
And I haven't a trace — nor, indeed, any place
   For the dangerous vermiform.
      For I'm built on the strictest economy plan,
         And the model was made in a rush,
      While essaying to think almost drives me to drink,
         For I'm simply a mass of mush.

At night, when I slide on the sandy beach,
   And the moonbeams pierce me through,
The tears arise in my gelatine eyes
   And I gurgle a sob or two.
      For I wonder — ah, me!—in the time to come,
         When the days are no longer young,
      What fish's digestion will suffer congestion
         When the end of my song is sung.

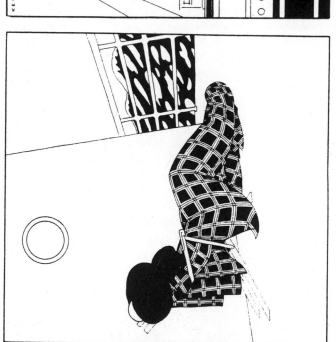

The Actress: A Mid-ocean Snapshot and a Dockside Pose for Camera Men

❧A Worldwind Tour in a Whirl

❧*Now that you've done everything and met everyone, you probably want to know something about all the special landmarks to look for on the seas and oceans you might come across on your cruise. Whether you're spending three days in the Caribbean, two weeks in the Mediterranean, or a year circling the globe, you'll run into something special, even if it's only an invisible line. In fact, since we're bound to offend somebody wherever we start, let's offend as many people as possible by starting at the International Dateline, where almost nobody lives and everybody talks about what they rarely think about (except in terms of years passing): time. Nicholas Coleridge put it succinctly: "Everyone agreed that if you were going to gain an extra day somewhere, right out of the blue, it couldn't have happened in a more interesting place, right out in the blue." Mark Twain provides us with a more extended description of the effect an invisible line can have on one's life.*

Mark Twain
A Day Behind 1897

SEPT. 8 — *Sunday.* We are moving so nearly south that we cross only about two meridians of longitude a day. This morning we were in longitude 178 west from Greenwich, and 57 degrees west from San Francisco. To-morrow we shall be close to the center of the globe — the 180th degree of west longitude and 180th degree of east longitude.

And then we must drop out a day — lose a day out of our lives, a day never to be found again. We shall all die one day earlier than from the beginning of time we were foreordained to die. We shall be a day behindhand all through eternity. We shall always be saying to the other angels, "Fine day to-day," and they will be always retorting, "But it isn't to-day, it's to-morrow." We shall be in a state of confusion all the time and shall never know what true happiness is.

Next Day. Sure enough, it has happened. Yesterday it was September 8, *Sunday;* to-day, per the bulletin-board at the head of the companionway, it is September 10, *Tuesday*. There is something uncanny about it. And uncomfortable. In fact, nearly unthinkable, and wholly unrealizable, when one comes to consider it. While we were crossing the 180th meridian it was *Sunday* in the stern of the ship where my family were, and *Tuesday* in the bow where I was. They were eating the half of a fresh apple on the 8th, and I was at the same time eating the other half of it on the 10th — and I could notice how stale it was, already. The family were the same age that they were when I had left them five minutes before, but I was a day older now than I was then. The day they were living in stretched behind them half way round the globe, across the Pacific Ocean and America and Europe; the day I was living in stretched in front of me around the other half to meet it. They were stupendous days for bulk and stretch; apparently much larger days than we had ever been in before. All previous days had been but shrunk-up little things by comparison. The difference in temperature between the two days was very marked, their day being hotter than mine because it was closer to the equator.

Along about the moment that we were crossing the Great Meridian a child was born in the steerage, and now there is no way to tell which day it was born on. The nurse thinks it was Sunday, the surgeon thinks it was Tuesday. The child will never know its own birthday. It will always be choosing first one and then the other, and will never be able to make up its mind permanently. This will breed vacillation and uncertainty in its opinions about religion, and politics, and business, and sweethearts, and everything, and will undermine its principles, and rot them away, and make the poor thing characterless, and its success in life impossible. Every one in the ship says so. And this is not all — in fact, not the worst. For there is an enormously rich brewer in the ship who said as much as ten days ago, that if the child was born on his birthday he would give it ten thousand dollars to start its little life with. His birthday was Monday, the 9th of September.

If the ships all moved in the one direction — westward, I mean — the world would suffer a prodigious loss in the matter of valuable time, through the dumping overboard on the Great Meridian of such multitudes of days by ships' crews and passengers. But, fortunately, the ships do not all sail west, half of them sail east. So there is no real loss. These latter pick up all the discarded days and add them to the world's stock again; and about as good as new, too; for of course the salt water preserves them.

The Pacific Crossing is long and tedious, or extremely relaxing, depending on your point of view. An anonymous four-line poem sums it up:

> Straight Down
> *We haven't seen a sail so far,*
> *And it's hard to understand,*
> *For on this trip we always are*
> *Within five miles of land.*

The islands that dot and smudge the South Pacific are everything the painters and sit-coms tell you they are, well worth the Pacific Crossing, at least to some.

James J. Montague
South Sea Stuff

The Copra soars above the shores
   That pearl a sapphire sea.
And, like as not, a Hottentot
   Is waiting there for me.
The bay is calm, the fronded palm
   With lithe and sinuous grace
Bends o'er the maid and steeps in shade
   Her rather shadier face.
And if she stands upon the sands
   And wears that wistful smile
Till I appear, I sort of fear
   She'll be there quite a while.

Where tabus roam their island home
   With taafas on their brows,
Or dive through coves to pluck the loaves
   From sun-baked bread-fruit boughs,
For days and days a maiden's gaze
   Is fixed upon the blue
That she may mark my white-sailed bark
   That cleaves the atoll through.

I have not met the lady yet,
   And only wish her well,
But none the less I sort of guess
   She'll wait there quite a spell.

The paruu droops o'er dusky troops
   Of aborigines,
Who wait to hail the white man's sail
   Upon the tropic seas.
They're keen to wed, so we have read,
   And when his ship arrives,
With loving hearts they'll play the parts
   Of fond and loyal wives.
But if they wait to share my fate
   Beside the creaming foam,
They'll wait in vain — I'll tell 'em plain
   I'm quite content at home!

The Indian Ocean, the Persian Gulf, and the Suez Canal are waters you aren't likely to take a cruise in, but just in case you've got some ideas, you should listen to Jerome Weidman's experiences in the Suez Canal, a place you won't believe so many nations have fought over.

Jerome Weidman
Letter of Credit 1954

I AM not the most pleasant companion in the world. I cannot bear high temperatures. Once the mercury soars above ninety, I know there is just as much chance that I will forget my self-control as there is that I will remember it. I am not at my best in the summer. During July and August, even in New York where I am happiest, I am inclined to be short-tempered, irritable, and annoyingly inefficient. Even with this knowledge at my finger tips, it was not until I sailed through the Suez Canal in July that I realized how thoroughly impossible my conduct could become if I were subjected to enough heat. My irritation turned to rudeness. My temper became unreasonable. For perhaps twelve hours I was unbearable. When it was all over I was more astonished than contrite. To a certain extent, I still do not believe it. My apology is that I know of no other trip by conventional methods of transportation which makes you feel so certain that by the mere act of surviving until the end of the journey you have earned the right to a military decoration of high order.

When your ship creeps into the Canal at noon you are hanging over the rail, staring industriously in your anxiety not to miss a single detail of what you have been taught since childhood is one of the great engineering feats of all time. After some ten minutes of this, during which the ship has moved forward perhaps an eighth of a mile, you become aware suddenly that your eyeballs are not resting in their sockets in the manner to which you have become accustomed. You separate yourself from the rail and hurry into the lounge to glance at the thermometer.

The suspicion that started when your eyeballs began to smart and jump about is now confirmed by the thermometer and the small industrious trip hammer that starts to work steadily in the base of your skull. It is one hundred and two degrees in the shade. You were not in the shade during those first ten minutes on the rail. And if you have not already succeeded in lashing yourself firmly to a sizable case of sunstroke, you are close enough to it now to spoil your appetite for the rest of the Suez Canal. This places you approximately in the position of a character in *Beau Geste* who is lost in the Sahara and finds he has spoiled his appetite for sand. It is a trifle late to do anything about it.

You rush down to your cabin to soak your head in what was fairly cold water less than an hour before, and find that your basin taps seem to have been mysteriously connected with the vat into which all the leftover tea is tossed. You swallow two aspirin tablets and your hand comes away from your cheek soaking wet. You begin to realize that all the perspiring you have ever before done in your life has been so much amateur surface scratching. You put on a fresh pair of shorts and a clean shirt and find that the effort of changing your clothes has exhausted you so completely that you can scarcely stand up. You start to lie down on your bunk, but your reasoning processes are working just sufficiently to let you gather that this is the equivalent of boiling yourself in oil. You snatch a handful of handkerchiefs from your suitcase and stagger up on deck. By the time you get there the handkerchiefs are no longer fresh. Should the ship go aground at any moment during the next few hours, an event that seems disturbingly within the realm of probability, you are convinced, somewhat fantastically, that you have already accumulated enough perspiration in your handkerchiefs to float her free. You go into the bar and order a long drink.

"Ice, sir?" the barman, being English, asks.

You suppress the acidulous retort that comes to your lips. You are remembering your self-control.

"Yes," you say with an effort, "please."

Your voice sounds so loud and resonant that you feel you are addressing yourself inside an old boiler. You become aware of the extraordinary stillness. The ship does not seem to be moving. All motion appears to have ceased. Everybody has disappeared. As you walk out to the shady side of the deck you become aware that the other passengers have not disappeared at all. They are making the Canal passage in a horizontal position and their heads are hidden beneath the level of the deck chairs. This seems highly intelligent to you.

Thirty seconds after you decide to do likewise you discover that all the deck chairs are occupied. This does your temper no good whatsoever. You wander around the ship, hunting an empty deck chair or a bit of breeze, and find neither. You come back to the part of the deck from which you started and discover that you overlooked a long row of seven or eight chairs which have been empty all the time. What this does to your temper would reduce itself very nicely into a small but definitive dictionary of optimum profanity. The vague suspicion crosses your mind that your eyesight is failing rapidly and is dismissed as unimportant.

You drop into one of the vacant deck chairs. The canvas touches the bare skin of your thighs and arms in a searing caress. You ease yourself gingerly back into the chair and take a sip from the glass you have been carrying around for several minutes. All the ice has melted. The mixture reminds you of a bowl of soup that was once set before you in a restaurant just as you were called away to the telephone and to which you returned a quarter of an hour later. You hurl the drink overboard, glass and all, and rehearse a suitable remark for the steward who will reprimand you for willful destruction of the ship's property. You are beginning to forget the secret pride you used to take in your self-control. The glass lands in the Suez Canal with a slap so loud that once again you become aware of the crushing stillness. You start guiltily, sending a fine spray of loose perspiration flying in all directions. The oppressive silence settles down to a low, steady, inexplicable hum. Your mind darts back and forth, exploring nightmarish possibilities, until you realize with sudden horror that the humming sound can be caused by nothing but the pitiless, metallic glare of the pounding sun. You have a long, stabbing moment of terror.

One of the Indian college students comes along with a glass of beer in his hand. You know from experience that the beer is never served iced. At Suez Canal temperature it can scarcely be a pick-me-up. The sight of the beer in the sun makes you feel slightly nauseated. The Indian student is wearing a flannel blazer with the crest of his school embroidered on the left breast pocket. He smiles pleasantly.

"Beastly hot, isn't it?"

You don't answer. You remember that this is a long trip, that you will have to see him every day for more than a week. He sips the beer. You shudder.

"I just looked at the thermometer," he says. "One hundred and four in the shade."

He looks at you expectantly and you try to think of a suitable rejoinder.

"Centigrade?" you ask. "Or Fahrenheit?"

"I beg your pardon?"

You shake your head helplessly and smile wanly to indicate that what you said is unimportant, that you are too weak to repeat. He goes away. The luncheon gong sounds. You look at your wrist watch. The strap is soggy with perspiration. One o'clock. Eleven more hours to go. You will never last it through. Your bitter thoughts begin to alternate between guesses at the number of air-conditioned theatres, offices, and restaurants in New York, and the knowledge that nobody forced you to take this trip. It was your own idea. You are not like the other passengers who must get from one place to another for business or government reasons. You were a free agent. You did it with your eyes open. You were curious about the way people lived at the other side of the world. You were not content to satisfy your curiosity by reading a book. You wanted to look for yourself. A sardonic smile begins to twist your lips. The steward who is manipulating the luncheon gong is apparently dissatisfied with the response. He comes out on deck to stand immediately behind your chair and pound the gong. You don't move. He leans over you.

"Tiffin, sar?"

It takes a moment or two before you can trust yourself to speak.

"No," you say in a deadly monotone. "No tiffin."

The steward goes away and you remind yourself that you are going through the Suez Canal. You punch and push your mind through the haze of heat until it fastens for a while on the physical details about you. As the word "canal" shapes itself on your tongue you smile. If you had enough strength left you would chuckle. It occurs to you that calling this narrow ditch a canal is like calling a dripping faucet a tributary of the Mississippi. You know you are being unfair but you don't care. You are convinced that you get some small relief from the unbearable heat by being unfair to the Suez Canal. You don't know why, but you are in no condition to establish logical bases for your convictions. The ditch is so narrow that two ships cannot move along side by side. You recall vaguely that through no canal in the world do two ships move along side by side, but you erase the recollection from your mind. You are enjoying being unfair to the Suez Canal. The edges of the ditch are vague, undefined slopes of shifting sand. There is no snap, no smartness, no rigidity. There are no locks, no gleaming steel parts, no visible indications of modern engineering accomplishment. You can actually see the sand rolling down the slopes, sifting into the canal. Here and there the crawling ship passes a bit of concreted side, but even this does not keep the sand back. It pours steadily, relentlessly, over the concrete sides into the ditch. The whole thing has a homemade, schoolboy flavor. Something the children dug across a vacant lot after class on a rainy day. Occasionally the ship passes a dredging crew, a barge full of overworked natives glistening with sweat in the murderous sun as they scoop out the sand that is constantly flowing back. The ship is moving so slowly and the sand is sifting in so steadily that you begin to wonder if the Canal won't be blocked solidly before you get to the other end.

At two o'clock you go down to your cabin and return to the deck with a bath towel. Handkerchiefs are worthless. You mop for a while, then go into the bar and order a drink. You make a small bet with yourself about what the barman is going to say. You win.

"Ice, sir?"

You gather your wits for a crushing remark but realize you must hoard your energy for walking back out on deck again. You nod listlessly.

"Yes, ice."

You gulp the drink hastily and get it down before the ice melts. The sudden coolness makes you gasp. You order another. Before it is pushed out across the counter to you the effect of the first one has disappeared. You amuse yourself by trying to decide whether it is more sensible to sip slowly and get a prolonged modicum of faint coolness or gulp quickly and get a short, sharp, but real relief from the heat. The moments of indecision are fatal. By the time you put the glass to your lips the ice has melted. You return to your deck chair.

At three o'clock you are inventing bawdy limericks about Disraeli,

De Lesseps, and George Arliss. Even if they were good limericks they would be no relief from the singing heat. They are not good.

The man who is going out to Sumatra to take a job in the accounting department of an oil company drops into the deck chair next to yours. He tells you with excitement that if a ship goes aground in the Canal and remains stationary for more than twelve hours she is dynamited at once. He waits for you to ask why, but you don't. You wonder idly why you are not even remotely interested. He tells you. The toll charges for going through the Canal are so enormously heavy, and the number of vessels waiting to go through is so great, that it is cheaper to destroy the grounded vessel than to hold up the lucrative traffic. He waits for you to look startled. You are too exhausted to look even polite. You want to ask him where he picked up this choice bit of what sounds like shocking misinformation, but you lack the strength. You are telling yourself that it can't possibly get hotter. You are telling it to yourself with your tongue in your cheek. It gets hotter.

At four o'clock you become aware of a noisy clatter on the upper deck. You hear voices and laughter. A horrible suspicion flashes across your mind and you listen attentively. Unmistakably you hear the erratic tap of a ping-pong ball, the dull thud of a quoit. One hundred and four degrees in the shade and the Englishmen are continuing with the deck-sports tournament. The realization causes your stomach to fall away inside you like a trap door.

At five o'clock you try to read. The sun is beginning to bend in the sky. It should be getting cooler, but it doesn't. The lines of print dance up and down on the page. You stop trying to read and watch a native dhow sail by. Something clicks in your mind. If the dhow is able to sail by, there must be a breeze coming from somewhere. You sit up to look for the breeze and don't find it. But the effort of sitting up has forced your pores into additional activity and you go to work with your bath towel. You make an unsettling discovery. What you thought was a sudden and tender growth of beard proves to be a beautifully inflamed case of prickly heat. You are mildly impressed with the fact that you take the discovery with equanimity. The Indian college student comes along with his glass of beer. The flannel sports coat is plastered to his body and reminds you of a wet bath mat.

"Beastly hot, isn't it?"

You don't want to say what you would like to say, so you close your eyes and shake your head to indicate that you are worn out and do not feel in the mood for conversation. When you open your eyes he is still there. He looks at you unblinkingly for a moment, and then decides you must be joking. He is wrong.

"Ha, ha. But I say, really. Just looked at the thermometer again. One hundred and six in the shade. Seems unbelievable, doesn't it?"

"Not any more," you say.

At six o'clock the ship breaks into a sudden burst of activity. You tell yourself that you can't believe your eyes, but of course you are not being strictly honest. You can believe anything now, even that the sudden burst of excitement is caused by the Englishmen dressing for dinner. The sun is sinking fast now. A matter of common sense. You enter into a small argument with yourself. It's bound to get cooler. With the sun gone it can't possibly get hotter. A matter of common sense. With the sun gone, damn it, it *must* get cooler. At any rate, if it doesn't get cooler, certainly, at the very least, it won't get hotter. You go on like this for a while, wide awake to the fact that you are playing fast and loose with a full-grown case of hysteria. It gets hotter, of course, and when you see the Englishmen coming out on deck in their dinner coats and stiff white collars you start kicking your heels softly against the deck. The woman who is going out to Bombay to join her naval officer husband stops beside you to fan herself with a soggy copy of *Punch* and stare pointedly at your soaked shirt and sweat-stained khaki shorts.

"Rather on the sticky side, don't you think?"

"Quite," you say.

Oh, you're getting the hang of it, all right.

"Makes one wish one didn't have to go down to dinner, doesn't it?"

You nod and she bridles a bit. You aren't co-operating. She decides to abandon her skirmishing tactics and come out into the open.

"Won't you be going down to dinner at all?"

"Yes."

"Aren't you afraid you'll be a bit on the late side?"

"No."

"Surely, you're not going down in those . . . ?"

"Yes."

She is aghast. You are so drained of energy that you don't even feel pleased because she is aghast.

"Well, *really.*"

She sniffs and stalks away. You feel a twinge of remorse for your bad manners and realize that you are paying lip service to tradition. You see the Indian college student approaching. You can tell from his lope that he has been in conference with the thermometer again and you feel fairly certain that you don't have to be told it is hotter. You get out of your chair, stagger down to your cabin, bathe, change into fresh clothes, and stumble along to the dining salon. When you get there the fresh shirt is already stuck firmly to your back.

The dining room seems foggy with steam. The portholes are open and tin scoops have been stuck into them to catch the faintest hints of a breeze. There are no hints. You listen to the conversation around you and amuse yourself by speculating that if you had a dollar for every sentence over ten words that will be spoken about the heat between now and midnight you would be a wealthy man. The speculation ceases to be amusing when you realize that you are the sort of idiot whose first move, as soon as he put his hands on that money, would be to take a trip around the world, via the Suez Canal.

You push the food on your plate back and forth, making senseless geometric designs, and watch the stiff collars melting all around you, the splotches of perspiration working their way through the shoulder blades of the dinner jackets. You order ice cream for dessert and, when the Goanese steward sets it down before you, it slops over the sides of the saucer. He is too obsequiously deferential and apologetic as he mops up the horrible pink and brown liquid with a damp napkin.

At eight o'clock the huge searchlights are turned on. Everybody crowds to the upper decks to watch the wide beams of light cutting slowly across Asia Minor on your left and Africa on your right. Searchlights on sand and water are among the things that used to send your pulse leaping. Tonight they seem very dull. After several minutes you turn away. As you leave the rail the casual thought of a few minutes before comes back. Asia Minor on your left, Africa on your right. Two exotic continents, almost within touching distance of your outstretched hands. It should be an exciting thought. You try to whip your spirits to the pitch you had always been certain they would attain without help once you were in just this place. Your efforts prove a failure. It is not an exciting thought at one hundred and six degrees.

During the next two hours you change your shirt three times. At ten o'clock all the dinner jackets are soaked through, but the grim dancing continues. You decide that you need a change of venue and you go up to the top deck again, where the novelty of the searchlights has worn off sufficiently to send most passengers down to the dancing in the lounge. You give up trying to figure out how they stand it and warn yourself firmly not to conclude from this that they are not human. The huge searchlight beams poke through the stifling night, picking out the brackish water of the Suez Canal, the desert stretching away on either side, the sand sifting slowly down into the path of the ship. Occasionally the beam rests for a moment on a camel. The huge, ungainly animal stops to blink stupidly into the light. The man in the white turban and flowing robe who plods along beside him does not raise his head. With the bright blue sky studded with silver stars acting as a backdrop, the whole thing looks like a picture on a Christmas calendar.

The girl with the cauliflower ear who is going out to Penang, to marry her fiancé and live on a tin-mining estate, comes along and stops beside you. Yesterday you thought her shy and rather charming. Now, as you lean on the rail, it occurs to you that a girl with an ear like hers shouldn't wear her hair piled in a vivacious bun on the top of her head. You try to remember how she looked yesterday, but you cannot help wondering how she would react to your suggestion that she comb her hair forward and down over her face to form a sort of mask. She sighs audibly as she looks at the desert and the camel and the stars. You decide that the heat is too much for your gentlemanly instincts, you eliminate boxing as a possible source of that ear, and you wonder if she could have put in a season or two with a troupe of professional wrestlers. The searchlight picks out another camel, a glistening slice of the Suez Canal, a rolling piece of desert.

"The East," she sighs. "The East."

At eleven o'clock the Indian college student turns up from his latest assignation with the thermometer. You nod grimly when he tells you with excitement that the thermometer hasn't climbed at all for a full hour, and you suppress the suggestion that he do so instead.

At midnight the ship passes the lights of Suez and you are through. You feel a tingle of exultation. You suffer a moment of remorse for your temper and conduct during the past twelve hours, but you brush it aside. You will be remorseful tomorrow. Now you feel fine. You took quite a beating, but you managed to salvage something for your pride.

You're still on your feet.

&*The Mediterranean Sea is the center of the world even to people who live far away and have never visited its topless shores or wine-dark waters. It is the Odyssey, the Argonauts, the Evangelists, the Onasses. Since there is nothing prosaic about the Mediterranean or its most fabled little brothers, the Aegean and the Adriatic, here are two poems that celebrate the comic spirit of this most magical of all bodies of water.*

Sir Owen Seaman
The Schoolmaster Abroad

(The steam yacht Argonaut *was chartered from Messrs Perowne & Lunn by a body of public school masters for the purposes of an educative visit to the Levant)*

O 'Isles' (as Byron said) 'of Greece!'
   For which the firm of Homer sang,
Especially that little piece
   Interpreted by Mr Lang;
Where the unblushing Sappho wrote
The hymns we hardly like to quote; —

I cannot share his grave regret
   Who found your fame had been and gone;
There seems to be a future yet
   For Tenedos and Marathon;
Fresh glory gilds their deathless sun,
And this is due to Dr Lunn!

What though your harpers twang no more?
   What though your various lyres are dumb?
See where by Cirrha's sacred shore,
   Bold Argonauts, the Ushers come!
All bring their maps and some their wives,
And at the vision Greece revives!

The Delphic oracles are off,
   But still the site is always there;
The fumes that made the Pythian cough
   Still permeate the conscious air;
Parnassus, of the arduous 'grade',
May still be climbed, with local aid.

Lunching upon the self-same rock
   Whence Xerxes viewed the wine-red frith,
They realize with vivid shock
   The teachings of 'the smaller Smith';
With bated breath they murmur — 'This
Is actually Salamis!'

They visit where Penelope
   Nightly unwove the work of day,
Staving her suitors off till he,
   Ulysses, let the long-bow play,

And on his brave grass-widow's breast
Forgot Calypso and the rest.

In Crete, where Theseus first embraced
   His Ariadne, they explore
(Just now authentically traced)
   The footprints of the Minotaur;
And follow, to the maze's source,
The thread of some profound discourse.

That isle where Leto, sick with fright,
   So scandalized her mortal kin,
Where young Apollo, lord of light,
   Commenced his progress as a twin —
Fair Delos, they shall get to know,
And Paros, where the marbles grow.

Not theirs the course of crude delight
   On which the common tourist wends;
From faith they move, by way of sight,
   To knowledge meant for noble ends;
'Twill be among their purest joys
To work it off upon the boys.

One hears the travelled teacher call
   Upon the Upper Fifth to note
(Touching the Spartan counter-wall)
   How great the lore of Mr Grote;
And tell them, 'His are just the views
I formed myself — at Syracuse!"

When Jones is at a loss to show
   Where certain islands ought to be,
How well to whack him hard and low
   And say, 'The pain is worse for me,
To whom the Cyclades are quite
Familiar, like the Isle of Wight.'

And then the lecture after prep.!
   The Magic Lantern's lurid slide!
The speaker pictured on the step
   Of some old shrine, with no inside;
Or groping on his reverent knees
For Eleusinian mysteries!

Hellas defunct? O say not so,
　　While Public School-boys faint to hear
The tales of antique love or woe,
　　Brought home and rendered strangely clear
With instantaneous Kodak-shots
Secured by Ushers on the spots!

Phyllis Hartnoll
Overdose of Islands 1968

I have visited too many islands
　　I am hot and untidy and cross,
And I cannot distinguish between them
　　For all of them ended in -os.

And each one was famous for something —
　　Cos lettuce or Samian wine;
St. John had a vision on Patmos,
　　On Delos the lions were divine!
A girl was deserted on Naxos,
　　On Lesbos another wrote odes;
There was something uncanny at Knossos,
　　And something colossal at Rhodes.

The mountains rose straight from the sea-bed,
　　And the coaches roared up on the right
By vertiginous roads without fences
　　And never a lay-by in sight.
For the trouble with islands is transport —
　　The buses are hell in the heat,
Bestriding a donkey needs practice,
　　And ruins just ruin the feet.

So set me a chair on the sun-deck,
　　With ice tinkling into my glass;
And if we sight any more islands
　　I will spare them a glance as they pass.

❧No matter how romantic the Mediterranean may be, it is the Atlantic Ocean that links North America with its Great Mother Britain and her little coterie, known to the world as Europe. It is across this expanse that America sends its Rhodes Scholars, troops, and, once *upon a time, bargain-hunters. It is across this expanse that Britain sends Her scientists, nannies, and cultural TV hosts. But what with all this high-tech exporting and importing, what's in it for the cruisemate who's decided to escape the airline fare wars and go in style? Rhodes Scholar Christopher Morley has a few words to share with you.*

Christopher Morley
That Subtle Change *c1930*

THE following day there was that subtle change that comes over every Atlantic voyage about three quarters of the way across. Perhaps it happens at the place where the waves are parted, like hair. For on one side you see them rolling in toward America; on the other they move with equal regularity toward England and France. So obviously there must be a place where they turn back to back. The feeling of Europe being near increased the humility of passengers making their maiden voyage; more than ever they shrank from the masterful condescension of those anxious to explain what an intolerable thrill the first sight of Land's End would be. A certain number of English ladies, who had lain mummified and plaided in their chairs, now began to pace the deck like Britannia's daughters. Even one or two French, hitherto almost buried under the general mass of Anglo-Saxon assertiveness, pricked up and showed a meagre brightness. The young women with the phonograph, if they had been listening, might now have learned how to pronounce Cherbourg. Friendships that had been still a trifle green and hard suddenly ripened and even fell squashily overripe. Champagne popped in the dining saloon; the directors of Messrs. Bass prepared to declare another dividend; there was a fancy-dress ball. A homeward-bound English lecturer hoped that the weather would be clear going up the Chops of the Channel; for then, he said, in the afternoon light you will see the rocks of Cornwall shining like opals. But the weather grew darker and wetter; and with every increase of moisture and gale the British passengers grew ruddier and more keen. Even the breakfast kippers seemed stronger, more pungent, as they approached their native waters; the grapefruit correspondingly pulpier and less fluent. It was borne in upon the Americans that they were now a long way from home. Hardheaded business men, whose transactions with the smokeroom steward now proved to have had some uses, were showing their wives how to distinguish the half-crown from the florin. It struck them oddly that it might be some time before they would see again the Detroit *Free Press* or the Boston *Transcript*. Thus, in varying manners, came the intuition (which always reaches the American with a peculiar shock) that they were approaching a different world — a world in which they were only too likely to be regarded as spoiled and plunderable children. The young women with the phonograph, subconsciously resenting this, kept the records going prodigiously.

&The Caribbean, like the Mediterranean, seems to have been designed for cruising and spelling bees. The principal difference is that the Caribbean has a history we aren't taught in school or place of worship (at least after Columbus happened upon it). In fact, as the story is told by travel writer Harry Franck, "When the queen asked for a description of [Puerto Rico], Columbus crumpled up a sheet of paper and, tossing it upon the table, cried, 'It looks just like that, your Majesty!' " Not quite Homer describing Ithaca, but certainly more to the point. Rather than in classics and scriptures, we discover the Caribbean in the adventure books we take under the covers as children and in the colonialist, multigenerational novels we skim in our easychairs as adults. Not high literature, perhaps, but no less enjoyable for that.*

A trip to the Caribbean from the Friendly Uncle to the north includes such special events as entering the Gulf Stream, sighting the Southern Cross, and watching the water get more and more Caribbean.

James Steele
The Gulf Stream 1881

F INALLY, the time came for us to cross the Gulf Stream. It was almost the last thing we did on that voyage. It reminds me that you cannot go into a company of intelligent people anywhere, and ask a question about this celebrated current just for something to say, but that three or four of them will be ready to tell you all about it, while the rest look pityingly at the spectacle of ignorance exhibited by you in these days of free schools and cheap "institutes." Everybody knows all about it. But having been through and over and across it a great many times, I have really grown unsettled in my opinions with regard to it. The boundaries of its ink-blue waters are so well defined that one can see the stem in the sea and the stern in the stream. It is deep, warm, and of vaster volume than all the rivers combined. Where does it have its source, and what mysterious gravitation causes its ceaseless and mighty flow? Why do its tepid waters refuse to mingle with the others? Whence does it come, and whither go? What *causes* it? It was explained when it was first discovered, and has been quite well understood ever since. The explanations have all been specially constructed to suit the fact. But, in spite of it all, it leaves the impression that it is an unsolved mystery. We know what it does, and the good it does, and what an illustration it is of the wisdom, goodness, and perpetual care of the Creator. I have no theories to advance upon the subject. I only know it is there, a gigantic warming apparatus for one-half of the civilized world.

Mark Twain
The Southern Cross 1897

WE are moving steadily southward — getting further and further down under the projecting paunch of the globe. Yesterday evening we saw the Big Dipper and the north star sink below the horizon and disappear from our world. No, not "we," but they. They saw it — somebody saw it — and told me about it. But it is no matter, I was not caring for those things. I am tired of them, anyway. I think they are well enough, but one doesn't want them always hanging around. My interest was all in the Southern Cross. I had never seen that. I had heard about it all my life, and it was but natural that I should be burning to see it. No other constellation makes so much talk. I had nothing against the Big Dipper — and naturally couldn't have anything against it, since it is a citizen of our own sky, and the property of the United States — but I did want it to move out of the way and give this foreigner a chance. Judging by the size of the talk which the Southern Cross had made, I supposed it would need a sky all to itself.

But that was a mistake. We saw the Cross tonight, and it is not large. Not large, and not strikingly bright. But it was low down toward the horizon, and it may improve when it gets up higher in the sky. It is ingeniously named, for it looks just as a cross would look if it looked like something else. But that description does not describe; it is too vague, too general, too indefinite. It does after a fashion suggest a cross — a cross that is out of repair — or out of drawing; not correctly shaped. It is long, with a short cross-bar, and the cross-bar is canted out of the straight line.

It consists of four large stars and one little one. The little one is out of line and further damages the shape. It should have been placed at the intersection of the stem and the cross-bar. If you do not draw an imaginary line from star to star it does not suggest a cross — nor anything in particular.

One must ignore the little star, and leave it out of the combination — it confuses everything. If you leave it out, then you can make out of the four stars a sort of cross — out of true; or a sort of kite — out of true; or a sort of coffin — out of true.

Lafcadio Hearn
Bluer and Bluer:
Into the Caribbean 1900

WE steam under the colossal span of the mighty bridge; then for a little while Liberty towers above our passing, — seeming first to turn towards us, then to turn away from us, the solemn beauty of her passionless face of bronze. Tints brighten; — the heaven is growing a little bluer. A breeze springs up. . . .

Then the water takes on another hue: pale-green lights play through it. It has begun to sound. Little waves lift up their heads as though to look at us, — patting the flanks of the vessel, and whispering to one another.

Far off the surface begins to show quick white flashes here and there, and the steamer begins to swing. . . . We are nearing Atlantic waters. The sun is high up now, almost overhead: there are a few thin clouds in the tender-colored sky, — flossy, long-drawn-out, white things. The horizon has lost its greenish glow: it is a spectral blue. Masts, spars, rigging, — the white boats and the orange chimney, — the bright deck-lines, and the snowy rail, — cut against the colored light in almost dazzling relief. Though the sun shines hot the wind is cold: its strong irregular blowing fans one into drowsiness. Also the somnolent chant of the engines — *do-do,hey! do-do, hey!* — lulls to sleep.

. . . Towards evening the glaucous sea-tint vanishes, — the water becomes blue. It is full of great flashes, as of seams opening and reclosing over a white surface. It spits spray in a ceaseless drizzle. Sometimes it reaches up and slaps the side of the steamer with a sound as of a great naked hand. The wind waxes boisterous. Swinging ends of cordage crack like whips. There is an immense humming that drowns speech, — a humming made up of many sounds: whining of pulleys, whistling of riggings, flapping and fluttering of canvas, roar of nettings in the wind. And this sonorous medley, ever growing louder, has rhythm, — a *crescendo* and *diminuendo* timed by the steamer's regular swinging: like a great Voice crying out, "Whoh-oh-oh! whoh-oh-oh!" We are nearing the life-centres of winds and currents. One can hardly walk on deck against the ever-increasing breath; — yet now the whole world is blue, — not the least cloud is visible; and the perfect transparency and voidness about us make the immense power of this invisible medium seem something ghostly and awful . . . The log, at every revolution, whines exactly like a little puppy; — one can hear it through all the roar fully forty feet away . . .

MORNING: The second day. The sea is an extraordinary blue, — looks to me something like violet ink. Close by the ship, where the foam-clouds are, it is beautifully mottled, — looks like blue marble with exquisite veinings and nebulosities . . . Tepid wind, and cottony white clouds, — cirri climbing up over the edge of the sea all around. The sky is still pale blue, and the horizon is full of a whitish haze.

. . . A nice old French gentleman from Guadeloupe presumes to say this is not blue water; — he declares it greenish *(verdâtre)*. Because I cannot discern the green, he tells me I do not yet know what blue water is. *Attendez un peu!* . . .

. . . The sky-tone deepens as the sun ascends, — deepens deliciously. The warm wind proves soporific. I drop asleep with the blue light in my face — the strong bright blue of the noonday sky. As I doze it seems to burn like a cold fire right through my eyelids. Waking up with a start, I fancy that everything is turning blue, — myself included. "Do you not call this the real tropical blue?" I cry to my French fellow-traveller. *"Mon Dieu! non,"* he exclaims, as in astonishment at the question; — "this is not blue!" . . . What can be *his* idea of blue, I wonder!

Clots of sargasso float by, — light-yellow sea-weed. We are nearing the Sargasso-sea, — entering the path of the trade-winds. There is a long ground-swell, the steamer rocks and rolls, and the tumbling water always seems to me growing bluer; but my friend from Guadeloupe says that this color "which I call blue" is only darkness — only the shadow of prodigious depth.

Nothing now but blue sky and what I persist in calling blue sea. The clouds have melted away in the bright glow. There is no sign of life in the azure gulf above, nor in the abyss beneath; — there are no wings or fins to be seen. Towards evening, under the slanting gold light, the color of the sea deepens into ultramarine; then the sun sinks down behind a bank of copper-colored cloud.

MORNING of the third day. Same mild, warm wind. Bright blue sky, with some very thin clouds in the horizon, — like puffs of steam. The glow of the sea-light through the open ports of my cabin makes them seem filled with thick blue glass . . . It is becoming too warm for New York clothing . . .

Certainly the sea has become much bluer. It gives one the idea of liquefied sky: the foam might be formed of cirrus clouds compressed — so extravagantly white it looks to-day, like snow in the sun. Nevertheless, the old gentleman from Guadeloupe still maintains this is not the true blue of the tropics!

. . . The sky does not deepen its hue to-day: it brightens it; — the blue glows as if it were taking fire throughout. Perhaps the sea may deepen its hue; — I do not believe it can take more luminous color without being set aflame. . . . I ask the ship's doctor whether it is really true that the West Indian waters are any bluer than these. He looks a moment at the sea, and replies, "*Oh yes!*" There is such a tone of surprise in his "oh" as might indicate that I had asked a very foolish question; and his look seems to express doubt whether I am quite in earnest . . . I think, nevertheless, that this water is extravagantly, nonsensically blue!

I read for an hour or two; fall asleep in the chair; wake up suddenly; look at the sea, — and cry out! This sea is impossibly blue! The painter who should try to paint it would be denounced as a lunatic . . . Yet it is transparent; the foam-clouds, as they sink down, turn sky-blue, — a sky-blue which now looks white by contrast with the strange and violent splendor of the sea color. It seems as if one were looking into an immeasurable dyeing vat, or as though the whole ocean had been thickened with indigo. To say this is a mere reflection of the sky is nonsense! — The sky is too pale by a hundred shades for that! This must be the natural color of the water, — a blazing azure, — magnificent, impossible to describe.

AND the fourth day. One awakens unspeakably lazy; — this must be the West Indian languor. Same sky, with a few more bright clouds than yesterday; — always the warm wind blowing. There is a long swell. Under this trade-breeze, warm like a human breath, the ocean seems to pulse, — to rise and fall as with a vast inspiration and expiration. Alternately its blue circle lifts and falls before us and behind us; — we rise very high; we sink very low, — but always with a slow long motion. Nevertheless, the water *looks* smooth, perfectly smooth; the billowings which lift us cannot be seen; — it is because the summits of these swells are mile-broad, — too broad to be discerned from the level of our deck.

. . . Ten A.M. — Under the sun the sea is flaming, dazzling lazulite. My French friend from Guadeloupe kindly confesses this is *almost* the color of tropical water. . . . Weeds floating by, a little below the surface, are azured. But the Guadeloupe gentleman says he has seen water still more blue. I am sorry, — I cannot believe him.

A State Of Vacancy

"*D*on't you nor any other friend of mine never go to sleep with his head in a ship anymore."

The other man gave a grunt of discontented acquiescence, turned over in his berth, and drew his blanket over his head.

"For," said Mr. Tapley, pursuing the theme by way of soliloquy, in a low tone of voice, "the sea is as nonsensical a thing as any going. It never knows what to do with itself. It hasn't got no employment for its mind, and is always in a state of vacancy. Like them Polar bears in the wild-beast shows as is constantly a-nodding their heads from side to side, it never *can* be quiet. Which is entirely owing to its uncommon stupidity." — *Charles Dickens, from* Martin Chuzzlewit, *1844.*

"Now I suppose we can look forward to a reunion with this crowd every year for the rest of our lives."

THE HOME STRETCH

❧Stories

❧*Before we take you back to your home port, we would like to pay homage to the other gods of the sea, the Muses. Storytelling is the way of the waves, the mortar that has always held together all those men who have spent months and years in the middle of a tossing desert, the thing that's made sailors and their passengers laugh so hard they finally filled the shallow lake up to its brim with saltwater tears. Of course, according to this last theory we have not only the melting of the polar ice-caps to worry about, but also the reading of this book. But it's too late now, so you might as well read the following tales of the sea, by a hodgepodge of writers that includes Somerset Maugham, Wolcott Gibbs, Stanley Ross, Pierre Loving, R. G. G. Price, and Michael A. Musmanno.*

Stanley Ross
Cruising 1981

MIAMI Saturday. It pouring. It not supposed to. This Sunshine State not Monsoon Miami. Wipers pack up. Taxi hardly drive. Arrive docks. Go up long steps. Called gangplank. Sound vaguely rude. Big hold-up. Think old lady bad leg. Think most passengers bad leg. Some never seem move unless prod. Think maybe hospital ship. Cruise begin look like bundle fun. Go cabin. What this? Free champagne? Daddy always taught no such thing free lunch. Still champagne not lunch, unless you earl. Me not earl, only poor bond dealer. Look bottle. Suspicious. Think Pomaigne. Wife disagree. She want show tender loving care. So open instead me. Explode in face. Wife face thank God. Eye swell like pingpong ball. Look like Rocky Marciano after title fight. Wife say let go home now or buy diamond eye-patch. Think will sue boat. No warning exploding bottles. Tell doctor will want million dollars. Wife prepared weeks for trip. New clothes cost fortune. Hair coloured. Skin coloured. Now got nice big coloured eye.

It nice having wife black eye. Feel quite hero. Everyone thinks beat wife. Passengers nudge when go by. Women give dirty looks. Men mutter words wives not hear. Attaboy, stuff women's lib. etc. Meet captain cocktail party. Tell him lawyer take case. He not impressed. Don't think he hear what say. Don't think he hear what anyone say. Say it louder. He smile, turn away. Think another loony passenger. So miss photo with great man. Wife mad. Everyone got photo with captain. Everyone bound notice we not on wall with other thousand pictures.

It rough. It not supposed be rough. This Caribbean cruise where sun all day, sea like pond. Coloured lights round afterdeck. Steel band play all night. But boat go up, down like big dipper. Want lay down. Wife want eat. Say hungry. Put on big dark glasses, look mysterious. Go dining room. I lay on bed. Look at banana. Banana look at me. I angry wife gone, so bite banana. It struggle. It go down fighting. It still fighting inside. Sit up. Wonder who going win. Think not me.

Stand up. Boat stand on head. Fall down. Hurt bum on side bed. Think want go home. Glad on hospital ship. Wonder if do diamond bum patch. Must do, Americans buy anything. Limp down slow. Now just like other passengers. Wife not in dining-room. In bar laughing three men. Should have known. Wife not jump up kiss me, say who a brave chap then. Look cold at me. Announce loud "he seasick". Feel unnecessary.

Go dining-room. Waiter surprised see us. Lazy bugger. He happy it rough. No work. He say first time ever known captain order not lay breakfast. Must be going have gale. What he talking about. Already gale. Think bleeding hurricane. Wish not seen *Poseidon Adventure*. Look at ceiling. Wonder what can hold if boat go upside down. Look for little boy tell me how find airshaft. Get frightened. No little boy. Only old people. Ask wife where little boys are. Wife want know what hell talking about. Tell her. Wife look at me long time. Put on patient voice. You tired she say. Why not go bed. She take 50 dollars. Go play blackjack. Sit wonder why I come. She come back late. Great fistful chips. All hers now. Mine lost first few hands. Annoyed had use own money. Call me cheapskate.

Next day San Blas island. Must be Wednesday. People primitive, pee in backyard. Women rings through noses. Wife want buy this, want buy that. Think have ring through own nose. Now know why I come. Old crone thrusts child at wife. Screams, "Take picture, give money." Monkey lands on shoulder. Heart nearly jump through ear. Monkey grab camera. Child hit wife in face. Please God not other eye. Grab camera back. Monkey bite finger. Rush boat tender. Back ship, chop-chop. Scream, "Rabies." Doctor give jab unbruised side of bum. He sarcastic. Ask if now going sue monkey. This only five days. Decide not strong enough world cruise. Wonder if ship have coffin maker. Only ten more days. Decide start pack. Bond dealing piece cake compared cruising. Hope make it home.

Somerset Maugham
Mr. Know-All c1927

I WAS prepared to dislike Max Kelada even before I knew him. The war had just finished and the passenger traffic in the ocean-going liners was heavy. Accommodation was very hard to get and you had to put up with whatever the agents chose to offer you. You could not hope for a cabin to yourself and I was thankful to be given one in which there were only two berths. But when I was told the name of my companion my heart sank. It suggested closed portholes and the night air rigidly excluded. It was bad enough to share a cabin for fourteen days with anyone (I am going from San Francisco to Yokohama), but I should have looked upon it with less dismay if my fellow passenger's name had been Smith or Brown.

When I went on board I found Mr. Kelada's luggage already below. I did not like the look of it; there were too many labels on the suitcases, and the wardrobe trunk was too big. He had unpacked his toilet things, and I observed that he was a patron of the excellent Monsieur Coty; for I saw on the washing-stand his scent, his hairwash and his brilliantine. Mr. Kelada's brushes, ebony with his monogram in gold, would have been all the better for a scrub. I did not at all like Mr. Kelada. I made my way into the smoking-room. I called for a pack of cards and began to play patience. I had scarcely started before a man came up to me and asked me if he was right in thinking my name was so and so.

"I am Mr. Kelada," he added with a smile that showed a row of flashing teeth, and sat down.

"Oh, yes, we're sharing a cabin, I think."

"Bit of luck, I call it. You never know who you're going to be put in with. I was jolly glad when I heard you were English. I'm all for us

English sticking together when we're abroad, if you understand what I mean."

I blinked.

"Are you English?" I asked, perhaps tactlessly.

"Rather. You don't think I look like an American, do you? British to the backbone, that's what I am."

To prove it, Mr. Kelada took out of his pocket a passport and airily waved it under my nose.

King George has many strange subjects. Mr. Kelada was short and of a sturdy build, clean-shaven and dark skinned, with a fleshy, hooked nose and very large, lustrous and liquid eyes. His long black hair was sleek and curly. He spoke with a fluency in which there was nothing English and his gestures were exuberant. I felt pretty sure that a closer inspection of that British passport would have betrayed the fact that Mr. Kelada was born under a bluer sky than is generally seen in England.

"What will you have?" he asked me.

I looked at him doubtfully. Prohibition was in force and to all appearance the ship was bone dry. When I am not thirsty I do not know which I dislike more, ginger ale or lemon squash. But Mr. Kelada flashed an oriental smile at me.

"Whisky and soda or a dry martini, you have only to say the word."

From each of his hip pockets he fished a flask and laid it on the table before me. I chose the martini, and calling the steward he ordered a tumbler of ice and a couple of glasses.

"A very good cocktail," I said.

"Well, there are plenty more where that came from, and if you've got any friends on board, you tell them you've got a pal who's got all the liquor in the world."

Mr. Kelada was chatty. He talked of New York and of San Francisco. He discussed plays, pictures, and politics. He was patriotic. The Union Jack is an impressive piece of drapery, but when it is flourished by a gentleman from Alexandria or Beirut, I cannot but feel that it loses somewhat in dignity. Mr. Kelada was familiar. I do not wish to put on airs, but I cannot help feeling that it is seemly in a total stranger to put mister before my name when he addresses me. Mr. Kelada, doubtless to set me at my ease, used no such formality. I did not like Mr. Kelada. I had put aside the cards when he sat down, but now, thinking that for this first occasion our conversation had lasted long enough, I went on with my game.

"The three on the four," said Mr. Kelada.

There is nothing more exasperating when you are playing patience than to be told where to put the card you have turned up before you have had a chance to look for yourself.

"It's coming out, it's coming out," he cried. "The ten on the knave."

With rage and hatred in my heart I finished. Then he seized the pack.

"Do you like card tricks?"

"No, I hate card tricks," I answered.

"Well, I'll just show you this one."

He showed me three. Then I said I would go down to the dining-room and get my seat at table.

"Oh, that's all right," he said. "I've already taken a seat for you. I thought that as we were in the same stateroom we might just as well sit at the same table."

I did not like Mr. Kelada.

I not only shared a cabin with him and ate three meals a day at the same table, but I could not walk round the deck without his joining me. It was impossible to snub him. It never occurred to him that he was not wanted. He was certain that you were as glad to see him as he was to see you. In your own house you might have kicked him downstairs and slammed the door in his face without the suspicion dawning on him that he was not a welcome visitor. He was a good mixer, and in three days knew everyone on board. He ran everything. He managed the sweeps, conducted the auctions, collected money for prizes at the sports, got up quoit and golf matches, organized the concert and arranged the fancy-dress ball. He was everywhere and always. He was certainly the best hated man in the ship. We called him Mr. Know-All, even to his face. He took it as a compliment. But it was at mealtimes that he was most intolerable. For the better part of an hour then he had us at his mercy. He was hearty, jovial, loquacious and argumentative. He knew everything better than anybody else, and it was an affront to his overweening vanity that you should disagree with him. He would not drop a subject, however unimportant, till he had brought you round to his way of thinking. The possibility that he could be mistaken never occurred to him. He was the chap who knew. We sat at the doctor's table. Mr. Kelada would certainly have had it all his own way, for the doctor was lazy and I was frigidly indifferent, except for a man called Ramsay who sat there also. He was as dogmatic as Mr. Kelada and resented bitterly the Levantine's cocksureness. The discussions they had were acrimonious and interminable.

Ramsay was in the American Consular Service and was stationed at Kobe. He was a great heavy fellow from the Middle West, with loose fat under a tight skin, and he bulged out of his ready-made clothes. He was on his way back to resume his post, having been on a flying visit to New York to fetch his wife who had been spending a year at home. Mrs. Ramsay was a very pretty little thing, with pleasant manners and a sense of humour. The Consular Service is ill paid, and she was dressed always very simply; but she knew how to wear her clothes. She achieved an effect of quiet distinction. I should not have paid any particular attention to her but that she possessed a quality that may be common enough in women, but nowadays is not obvious in their demeanour. You could not look at her without being struck by her modesty. It shone in her like a flower on a coat.

One evening at dinner the conversation by chance drifted to the subject of pearls. There had been in the papers a good deal of talk about the culture pearls which the cunning Japanese were making, and the doctor remarked that they must inevitably diminish the value of real ones. They were very good already; they would soon be perfect. Mr. Kelada, as was his habit, rushed the new topic. He told us all that was to be known about pearls. I do not believe Ramsay knew anything about them at all, but he could not resist the opportunity to have a fling at the Levantine, and in five minutes we were in the middle of a heated argument. I had seen Mr. Kelada vehement and voluble before, but never so voluble and vehement as now. At last something that Ramsay said stung him, for he thumped the table and shouted:

"Well, I ought to know what I am talking about. I'm going to Japan just to look into this Japanese pearl business. I'm in the trade and there's not a man in it who won't tell you that what I say about pearls goes. I know all the best pearls in the world, and what I don't know about pearls isn't worth knowing."

Here was news for us, for Mr. Kelada, with all his loquacity, had never told anyone what his business was. We only knew vaguely that he was going to Japan on some commercial errand. He looked round the table triumphantly.

"They'll never be able to get a culture pearl that an expert like me can't tell with half an eye." He pointed to a chain that Mrs. Ramsay wore. "You take my word for it, Mrs. Ramsay, that chain you're wearing will never be worth a cent less than it is now."

Mrs. Ramsay in her modest way flushed a little and slipped the chain inside her dress. Ramsay leaned forward. He gave us all a look and a smile flickered in his eyes.

"That's a pretty chain of Mrs. Ramsay's, isn't it?"

"I noticed it at once," answered Mr. Kelada. "Gee, I said to myself, those are pearls all right."

"I didn't buy it myself, of course. I'd be interested to know how much you think it cost."

"Oh, in the trade somewhere round fifteen thousand dollars. But if it was bought on Fifth Avenue I shouldn't be surprised to hear that anything up to thirty thousand was paid for it."

Ramsay smiled grimly.

"You'll be surprised to hear that Mrs. Ramsay bought that string at a department store the day before we left New York, for eighteen dollars."

Mr. Kelada flushed.

"Rot. It's not only real, but it's as fine a string for its size as I've ever seen."

"Will you bet on it? I'll bet you a hundred dollars it's imitation."

"Done."

"Oh, Elmer, you can't bet on a certainty," said Mrs. Ramsay.

She had a little smile on her lips and her tone was gently deprecating.

"Can't I? If I get a chance of easy money like that I should be all sorts of a fool not to take it."

"But how can it be proved?" she continued. "It's only my word against Mr. Kelada's."

"Let me look at the chain, and if it's imitation I'll tell you quickly enough. I can afford to lose a hundred dollars," said Mr. Kelada.

"Take it off, dear. Let the gentleman look at it as much as he wants."

Mrs. Ramsay hesitated a moment. She put her hands to the clasp.

"I can't undo it," she said. "Mr. Kelada will just have to take my word for it."

I had a sudden suspicion that something unfortunate was about to occur, but I could think of nothing to say.

Ramsay jumped up.

"I'll undo it."

He handed the chain to Mr. Kelada. The Levantine took a magnifying glass from his pocket and closely examined it. A smile of triumph spread over his smooth and swarthy face. He handed back the chain. He was about to speak. Suddenly he caught sight of Mrs. Ramsay's face. It was so white that she looked as though she were about to faint. She was staring at him with wide and terrified eyes. They held a desperate appeal; it was so clear that I wondered why her husband did not see it.

Mr. Kelada stopped with his mouth open. He flushed deeply. You could almost *see* the effort he was making over himself.

"I was mistaken," he said. "It's a very good imitation, but of course as soon as I looked through my glass I saw that it wasn't real. I think eighteen dollars is just about as much as the damned thing's worth."

He took out his pocketbook and from it a hundred-dollar bill. He handed it to Ramsay without a word.

"Perhaps that'll teach you not to be so cocksure another time, my young friend." said Ramsay as he took the note.

I noticed that Mr. Kelada's hands were trembling.

The story spread over the ship as stories do, and he had to put up with a good deal of chaff that evening. It was a fine joke that Mr. Know-All had been caught out. But Mrs. Ramsay retired to her stateroom with a headache.

Next morning I got up and began to shave. Mr. Kelada lay on his bed smoking a cigarette. Suddenly there was a small scraping sound and I saw a letter pushed under the door. I opened the door and looked out. There was nobody there. I picked up the letter and saw that it was addressed to Max Kelada. The name was written in block letters. I handed it to him.

"Who's this from?" He opened it. "Oh!"

He took out of the envelope, not a letter, but a hundred-dollar bill. He looked at me and again he reddened. He tore the envelope into little bits and gave them to me.

"Do you mind just throwing them out of the porthole?"

I did as he asked, and then I looked at him with a smile.

"No one likes being made to look a perfect damned fool," he said.

"Were the pearls real?"

"If I had a pretty little wife I shouldn't let her spend a year in New York while I stayed in Kobe," said he.

At that moment I did not entirely dislike Mr. Kelada. He reached out for his pocketbook and carefully put in it the hundred-dollar note.

Wolcott Gibbs
Cure 1937

M R. and Mrs. Graves, who had come on the cruise because
Mr. Graves had taken to whimpering in his sleep, were the
first at the table. Mr. Graves saw instantly that something was up.
Instead of the regular menu cards, there were great creamy folders
with pictures of Bermuda on their covers. There were six snappers—
those explosive paper cylinders, containing mottoes and "favors,"
that ornament children's parties—and a cardboard hat, with S. S.
Kursvaal printed on it, beside each place. Mr. Graves picked up his
hat and looked under it. There was nothing there. He had rather
expected a cobra.

"*Now* what the hell?" he said.

"It's the last night out," said Mrs. Graves. "They always have a
party then."

"Oh," said Mr. Graves.

"Perhaps you'd better put on your hat," she said gently. "Everybody seems to be doing it."

Looking around, Mr. Graves saw that this was true. The dining-
room was about half full, and all the guests were wearing cardboard
hats. It was, he felt, one of those occasions when it is best to con-
form. Mrs. Graves laughed.

"You look like the iceman's horse," she said.

By this time pandemonium had descended on the room. After putting on their hats, the guests had begun to apply themselves happily
to their snappers. The air was full of tiny explosions and the soft
squealing of ladies, deliciously terrified. The snappers contained
whistles and rattles and a sort of paper snake that unrolled with a
whinny when you blew into it. Mr. Graves pulled one of his snappers, and found a wooden pig with a whistle in its back. There was
also a slip of paper that said: "There'll be a hot time in the old town
tonight," instead of the usual scrap of inspirational verse. This
seemed grimly prophetic to Mr. Graves. He gathered up the five
remaining snappers and let them fall quietly under the table. Mr. and
Mrs. Tyler, who confessed that they did a lot to keep Milwaukee on
its toes socially, dropped into their seats across from the Graves.

"Hello, folks," said Mr. Tyler.

He had on a mess jacket, but he did not look especially like Clifton
Webb. He put on a cardboard hat, and so did Mrs. Tyler, who was a
large woman, rather casually assembled. Mrs. Tyler exploded one of

her snappers and found a collapsible wooden rattle that spread madness and desolation when put together and swung. She swung it with spirit. Mr. Tyler got a small tin whistle, but did better with it than might have been expected.

Miss Polly Canopy and the three Yale men appeared next and sat down, completing the table. The three Yale men had pursued Miss Canopy relentlessly throughout the cruise—catching her, Mrs. Tyler had remarked cynically, more often than not. One of the Yale men found a brass ring in his snapper and put it on Miss Canopy's finger.

"Make an honest woman of you," he said with a leer. Miss Canopy shrieked with rapture, but Mrs. Tyler only looked down her nose.

Somewhere near the end of the room, the orchestra blared into the "cruise song," the text of which appeared on a small card by each plate.

"Of all the ships that sail the sea,
   The Kursvaal is the ship for me.
   Though she's not an ocean liner,
   Not a ship that's built's built finer,"
thundered the passengers.

There was a lot more, ending in a nightmare of discords:
"On the ooooooold Kursvaaal."

Dishes began to appear before Mr. Graves. They were rich in color and eccentric in design, and he wondered vaguely if they were edible, although he had neither the spirit nor the appetite to find out. He would scarcely have had time in any case, because the steward was lit with a strange ecstasy of the occasion and put them down and took them away with great rapidity. For some reason he had on a high black hat with a capital "R" in white on both sides.

Miss Canopy and the Yale men yielded gaily to much champagne, and pelted each other with innuendoes which made it appear that Mrs. Tyler had underestimated Miss Canopy's activities, if anything. Mr. Tyler yearned toward Mr. Graves with a story about a policy he had sold to, by God, the toughest man in Wisconsin. Mrs. Tyler swung her grim rattle. Mrs. Graves, pink and beautiful, ate salted peanuts. From time to time everybody sang about the Kursvaal. Mr. Graves wished he were dead.

At a quarter to nine, one of the Yale men insulted Mrs. Tyler. She was, he said, staring at Miss Canopy like an odalisque.

"You're drunk," said Mrs. Tyler fiercely. "That girl, too. All four of you."

"Never mind, Mother," said Mr. Tyler, who would have made five if his wife had cared to be precise. "I'm going to smash somebody."

He had indeed risen to smash somebody when, without warning, the main lights in the room went out, leaving only a small, dim lamp on each table. In the half-light, strange things began to happen. The steward loomed suddenly beside Mr. Graves with a dish bearing a great damp block which gave off a frail and unearthly radiance.

"What's that?" demanded Mr. Graves uneasily.

"Ize-krim," said the steward.

Mr. Graves looked again, and indeed it was ice cream.

"Is ilictric lights inside," said the steward, thinking him still incredulous.

"Oh," said Mr. Graves. He declined the luminous ice cream, although Mr. and Mrs. Tyler and the undergraduates ate it without apparent discomfort. There was, by this time, such torment on Mr. Graves's face that his wife patted his knee under the table.

"Never mind, lamb," she said. "It's almost over. They certainly can't think of anything *more* to do to you."

"Oh, can't they?" said Mr. Graves darkly, and his pessimism was almost instantly justified. All the lights went out now, and in the darkness the orchestra burst once more into the cruise song. Suddenly across the room a row of fiery letters staggered into sight. They were large letters, suspended about six feet in the air, and although they wavered and blinked a good deal, it was soon apparent that they spelled KURSVAAL. The letters began a slow, bobbing circuit of the room, advancing implacably upon Mr. Graves.

"It's only the stewards," whispered Mrs. Graves, feeling her husband stiffen beside her as the fiery march approached. "They've got electric lights in their hats. Like the ice cream."

When the line came abreast of the table, he saw that this was true. In some manner electric lights had been installed inside the stewards' hats, and shone brightly through the transparent letters.

The fact that there was a reasonable explanation for the marching lights, however, did little to console Mr. Graves. It was too late. He knew miserably that they, and the illuminated ice cream, and the snappers, and even Miss Canopy and the Tylers, had already joined the long procession of disturbing images which came to torment his dreams. He would see them all many times at night, strangely illuminated from within and marching to that preposterous song, and he would still whimper.

"Come on," he said. "Let's get out of this."

Pierre Loving
The Crossing 1932

I

ALEXIS Kogan had made up his mind to give up the button business for good. The depression had, as he himself put it, hit him pretty hard, and he was far too soft-hearted to lower wages or discharge his workers. So he called into his office a few of the most intelligent of his operatives and announced in a weary voice that he was going to hand the business over to them. They could turn it, if they wished, into a kind of profit-sharing venture, a soviet, or they could sell it to his nearest competitor. As for himself, he didn't care. He was leaving for Europe on Saturday morning, and he didn't know when he would return.

The workers, both men and women, took over the business, elected committees, foremen and other officers. The factory was in Brooklyn and most of the employees lived in a section known as Brownsville. The air here was thick, the streets crowded and dirty; and so when the hot weather set in some of the members of the profit-sharing venture stayed away from the factory and took their families to the sea-shore at Coney Island. The business declined and wasted away, and finally it was sold for a song to Alexis Kogan's closest competitor, Jacob Greenwald of Greenwald and Feldstein.

But Alexis Kogan did not know what was the ultimate fate of the business he had built up slowly, year by year, over two decades, until he unexpectedly returned to New York; that is, stepped from the gangplank of the giant Cunarder at the foot of Fourteenth Street, when a long incoherent letter from his former employees was handed him. He glanced at the contents while waiting for his trunks and bags to be examined by the customs' inspector. Then he shoved it into his coat pocket.

In the meantime, however, between his renunciation of the business to his employees and his return to New York from Europe two months later, a whole life-time of inner experience and adventure had happened to Alexis Kogan.

II

Although this incident is of no great importance—that is, of significance in the interior life of Alexis Kogan, it was Mrs. Amelia Hibble who discovered the ghost on board the transatlantic liner during the eastward run. Her husband, Alfred Hibble, made an effort to soothe and placate her when amid hysterical sobs she tried to tell him exactly what happened on the previous night on deck.

"Take it easy," said Alfred Hibble to his wife, the next morning. "Don't carry on. It's very bad for you."

With a tired sigh, Mrs. Hibble slumped back into her bedberth. Her head was wrapped in turbanned compresses that had slipped away during her access of useless white rage at Mr. Hibble's inefficiency and native optimism. For several minutes she lay inert. Then very gently her husband said:

"Let's get the story right. The moon was out?"

"My God," moaned Mrs. Hibble. "Why bring in the moon?"

"Well, anyway, you don't mean what you say, do you? It wasn't — a ghost."

"It was!" insisted Mrs. Hibble, turning her face to the wall.

Alfred Hibble was thinking in his way: All this ghost business is applesauce. It had been a fine night, and on a trip like this there are always a lot of people wandering about on deck, for one reason or another. Couples murmuring behind exhausts and in the shadow of life-boats. Why bring in — ghosts?

The liner far out at sea had breathed, and was still breathing, like an immense animal. The engines down below hummed away, and the iron heart seemed to push steadily forward with only a low whirring vibration. They said she had four screws; but Alfred Hibble did not exactly know what that meant. The big liner just knew where she was going.

Alfred Hibble recalled the details of his wife's hysterical story: She couldn't sleep. Went up on deck. There wasn't much wind. Not enough to be bothered, anyway. No sentimental couples in sight. Nobody, in fact. She merely saw a watchman in the stern against a sky that slid down to the rim of the horizon with a cluster of hard bright stars.

A silhouette leaped out from nowhere. It leaped out and stopped in its tracks. It was rather lean and gangling. It blocked her away. What was it that made them collide? An unexpected roll of the boat perhaps.

Panic-stricken, Amelia Hibble fled, with the apparition close on her heels. It whipped after her into the dark empty lounge. She cast a frightened glance over her shoulder. The thing was thrashing its hands in a peculiar manner. The head was sort of wedge-shaped. The face was pale and distraught.

When she reached her cabin, Alfred was fast asleep in his

bedberth. She shot the bolt. Pantingly, as if this were not enough to keep the pursuer out, she heaved her shoulder against the door.

III

Although this had very little to do with the inner experience of Alexis Kogan, the following conversation, on the day after the episode chronicled above, took place between Alfred Hibble and a fellow-passenger, William Butterworth. They were pacing the promenade deck. The reclining passengers in their deck chairs looked up when they passed, from books or magazines, and noticed that their conversation was in earnest. Alfred Hibble was short and fat. William Butterworth was tall in bulk, and over his left eye, covering the temple among the roots of his greying hair, was a mouse-colored stain. Very early in their shipboard acquaintance both men had revealed their businesses and preferences. Alfred Hibble was in the lumber line in Michigan; William Butterworth manufactured doorknobs in Seattle Washington. Both occasionally enjoyed a game of poker and were proud of their golf.

Mr. Butterworth at one point in their peregrinations around the deck, said: "Well, you don't believe in ghosts, Mr. Hibble, do you now?"

"No I don't but — — —"

"You know women are peculiar."

"My steward has a theory — — —"

"Who wouldn't?"

"The steward," persisted Alfred Hibble, "says that maybe another passenger on board can't sleep. Has the same insomnia."

"Darned clever of him," Mr. Butterworth replied. "Any clues? This is getting thick — a crime mystery yarn, in fact. Who is it?"

"I can't say I know as yet."

"No doubt it's a swell Scotland Yard theory." Mr. Butterworth brushed some ash from his coat lapels. He pulled at his cigar. His eyes a bit oblique now, he put his hand half-confidentially on Alfred's lower shoulder. "You'll excuse me," he said, clearing his throat, "but I must see the little countess. She's waiting for me in the bar. You know — — —"

Alfred Hibble had limp gray eyes. He stared hard at Mr. Butterworth, slightly perplexed. His lower lip hung loose.

As Mr. Butterworth turned to leave him, he said with a knowing look at his timid companion: "My missus is playing bridge as usual."

Certainly Mr. Hibble's steward could have no traffic with the inner life of Alfred Kogan, ex-button manufacturer from Brooklyn, now on a pleasure trip to Europe. It was the first vacation he had taken in nearly twenty years. Yet it was the steward's English voice that just now made Alfred Hibble turn round abruptly. The familiar voice said:

"I beg your pardon, sir; but if you've a minute to spare. A half a second, sir. I'd like to have a word with you about last night's business." The steward calmly went on. "Have you seen the man yet?"

"My wife says it was a ghost." Alfred Hibble put in.

The steward smiled thinly. "As to that, sir, I can't say. But I have a theory. I have my suspicions. If you don't mind — — —"

He was a thick-set stocky man with a blond moustache, serious gray eyes and a pleasant Yorkshire accent.

"What do you think it is?" asked Alfred Hibble, eagerly.

"It's a gentleman on board. A gentleman with gray wavy hair. Hasn't been to a hairdresser for quite a while, I fancy. I had a talk with his steward. Habits most unusual, sir. Queer. You've seen him about. He's tall and thin, long-legged — you might say. Pale as milk in the face, sir. Having a bad time of it, but not biliousness. No, sir. I should say he's a bit worried-looking. Has his meals in his cabin. No, he's not squeamish. I believe he's our man, sir, and no mistake. Now I shouldn't be surprised if something, as you might say — if something he's done preyed on his mind, sir. My theory is — — —"

"You don't mean he's a criminal wanted by the police?"

"Good Lord, no, sir. But I've been on these boats over fifteen years, sir, and I'm used, as you might say, to the habits of gentlemen who travel. Sometimes it's rather hard on a married man — — — Some of 'em, especially from the States, acts queer at times. A bit odd-like. It isn't that booze that does it, either.

"People who travel, sir, are very much like kids on a holiday at the seashore. Or like a lot of factory-bolts let loose. It's the doing nothing that seems to start them off. Pop! they go. And then you can never guess the end of it. Doing nothing is of course what they find the hardest."

"What about this chap?" interrupted Alfred Hibble.

"Oh, he's just one of 'em. All this water around sometimes makes ladies and gentlemen cuckoo, as you say. The boat does all the work. The crew takes care of everything. And the passengers — well, we always do our best. We hope they have a good time. Now this gentleman of whom I was speaking — the one with the wavy hair — is an American-foreigner — — —"

"An American foreigner? What's that?"

"What I mean, sir, is that he's a Pole or a Roosian."

"I see."

"His steward says he's rich. He's talked to him about his business. Seems to have built up a tidy bit of fortune in the States. A smart gentleman, but a bit off, sir. Overwork is my theory. And Lord! a vacation on top of it all." He shook his head mournfully. There was an ominous look in his round solemn face.

Alfred Hibble thanked him and said: "Guess I'll go and tell my wife."

"One thing more, sir," the steward added. "The countess — — — The Italian lady — only she's not Italian at all, sir. American-Italian, sir, I fancy. Well, the countess says his business in the States is buttons. That's what she wanted me to tell you." Alfred Hibble, in spite of himself, raised his eyes in the direction of the bar. The steward went on: "She thought it would sort of help you out, sir, to know his business and all that."

"Did you say buttons?" Alfred asked, stopping indecisively with an absent look in his gaze.

"Yes, sir. Don't worry the lady, sir. She's had a bad time of it. I'll see what else I can find out."

"Thanks," Alfred murmured as the steward darted through a doorway.

V

Aileen Fentamiglia, the Italian-American countess, was very attractive; but of course, like nearly everybody else on board the Mermantia, she really had no point of contact with the upheaved inner life of Alexis Kogan. How could she? William Butterworth, while his wife was playing bridge or sitting in the warm sun on deck, liked to meet her in the bar. William Butterworth would invariably give his wife an extra tuck-in, bundling her cozily in her wraps and blankets, just before he went to meet Aileen Fentamiglia in the bar. They liked, both of them the idea of standing up and drinking. Aileen was slim and dark, lithe in her small expressive movements; and she had — as William Butterworth had early remarked — fine mercurial eyes. Her lips were rather fleshy, but curved finely. Her eyes held him and others. He told himself that they were quite remarkable, moving swiftly from gayety to half-intimations of mysterious pain, flickering at all times with an intense dark aliveness.

Aileen might easily have passed for an Italian of the south; but she was only Italian by marriage and, as she liked so much to say, by divorce. Since she had got rid of her husband, she volubly informed Mr. Butterworth, all the somnolent Italian in her makeup had risen to the surface.

"But you're a hundred-per cent American," Mr. Butterworth observed shrewdly in the bar. "Didn't you tell me you were born in Lake Forest?"

"Yes," said Aileen with wide-open innocent eyes. "But I am sure I was Italian in another incarnation."

"You told me, didn't you, that your name was Scott before your marriage?"

"Well, that's nothing. Incarnations change their nationalities when they are forced to cross borders or emigrate."

"Sounds good but — — —"

"Look what happens to Burgundy when it is exiled to England. Why, they call it claret. And *Fiori di Alpini* is *Edelweiss* in Germany."

"You're a clever kid," said Mr. Butterworth.

"Let's go out for a walk on deck," suggested Aileen. She eyed Mr. Butterworth closely, with a half-amused smile. "That is, if Mrs. Butterworth does not object," she added.

"Not at all — not at all."

They went out on deck. Then Mr. Butterworth steered Aileen up a gangway to the Hurricane deck where, as Aileen cunningly surmised, they would not be likely to run into Mrs. William Butterworth, swathed in her rugs and blankets with a drowsy book on her knees.

After two turns they decided to sit in a pair of empty chairs that stood in the lee of one of the huge red funnels. Aileen dangled her heavy jade bracelets over the arm of the chair, dangled them from beautifully carved slender wrists. Mr. Butterworth perceived how fine and tapering her fingers were; how well-kept and carmined her nails. He reached out and grasped her hand. The hand permitted itself to rest in his, as though oblivious to everything save its own secret thoughts.

The liner drummed smoothly under them, with only the faintest low vibration. The bright sun scalloped the mildly ruffled disc of the blue sea.

Suddenly Aileen spied Alfred Hibble some distance away, leaning over the rail. She withdrew her hand and called and waved to Alfred. He turned his head slowly, and when he saw who it was, he approached the two chairs in the lee of the huge funnel.

William Butterworth frowned.

Aileen's dark mobile eyes coquetted with Alfred Hibble. Alfred's expression was a mixture of pain and bewilderment.

"There's something I want to tell you, Mr. Hibble," she said.

Alfred's limp gray eyes questioned her. "It's worried me more than I can say, Mr. Hibble — this terrible business of your wife and the ghost. But I think I've found the true explanation at last. Didn't the steward tell you?"

Alfred mumbled a few words in affirmation.

"The mystery — if mystery it ever was — is solved at last, Mr. Hibble."

"Mystery — nonsense!" Mr. Butterworth blurted out. He pulled out a cigar and expertly lit it with his lighter.

"Do you know, it's that funny Mr. Kogan. Alexis Kogan is his name. He's just a scream — a wild wet scream. Really, I never saw anybody like him. Now listen — listen carefully, *mon cher,* and you'll be rewarded in the end. The second engineer — really a most charming fellow — he's just shown me over the whole boat. And he knows boats, believe me. He knows about people on boats, too, and that's more than most engineers can boast of. Whenever I meet an engineer who knows more about people than engines —"

"Don't trust him with any machinery," Mr. Butterworth cut in dryly. He puffed at his cigar, gazing stubbornly out to sea.

"Well, the engineer thinks — and I think too — that he's not all there. No —"

"Who?" asked Mr. Butterworth sharply.

"Why, our Alexis Kogan. I mean, of course, your wife's Alexis Kogan, Mr. Hibble — — —"

Alfred Hibble opened his eyes wide and his lips appeared to tremble.

"My wife's — — —?" he stammered.

"You know whom I mean. I get philosophical on trips like this, Mr. Hibble. Can't help it. I've crossed so often. Twelve times. Like my friend the engineer, I get to know, for example, that nearly all persons can be divided into land-people and boat-people. You see what I mean?"

Alfred Hibble nodded his head, although he did not quite unravel Aileen Fentamiglia's enigmatic words. He nodded his head, cast down his eyes shyly and pursed his lips, simply because on occasions like this it was his habit to do so. William Butterworth, looking very much bored, chewed the end of his cigar and drummed with his fists on the arms of his borrowed deck-chair.

"You see what I mean, Mr. Hibble?" Aileen lifted up her well-turned wrist and made a graceful gesture with her hand. "A boat-person is something unnatural — like a centaur, you know. He has tar, sea-weed and screw-oil in his system while on board; and a tiny foghorn in his head, tooting away. To wash it all clear, to drown it out, he consumes many cocktails or magnums of champagne. And usually he makes love to somebody who is not his wife." Mr. Butterworth stirred uneasily in his chair.

"Some," Aileen went on, "are just little tritons who blow their toy horns all day and all night. You know, they show off to the last pick-up on board — — — boasting what big shots they are back home. How the Rotary Club gave them a great send-off, and all that sort of thing."

"Yah?" said Mr. Butterworth, with unconcealed irony in his tone.

"Now, Mr. Kogan, who was born in Poland, is quite different. He doesn't sing his own praises. He's a modest man, very upset and rest-less. The fact is, he's a stowaway — — —"

"A stowaway!" exclaimed Alfred Hibble. "No, it's impossible."

"The fellow's got a lot of money," put in Mr. Butterworth.

"Well, he's not exactly that, off course," Aileen continued. "That's a shade off. It's really hard to explain him, or his boat-incar-nation. The point is he's a changed man, somehow. He's not him-self. He's been playing — well — ghost, but not with your wife. He's been doing it to scare himself."

"Rot — just plain rot!" exclaimed Mr. Butterworth. "Why don't you say he's cuckoo, and let it go at that, Aileen."

"No, that's not true. It wouldn't be right. Why, even the engineer admits that he's never seen so many people on the Mermantia trying to be something they just aren't."

"So?" Mr. Butterworth was by now very plainly annoyed.

"Now, Mr. Kogan," Aileen resumed, pointedly ignoring the door-knob manufacturer on her right, "is a prize case. Do you want to know something? He hasn't left this boat on two whole trips."

Mr. Butterworth catapulted himself into an upright posture and stared in baffled wonder at Aileen; then his gaze roamed over Alfred Hibble's calm face to see what effect the last words had upon the lit-tle fat man. Alfred Hibble's eyelashes fluttered uncertainly. Gradu-ally he raised his eyes and fixed them suspiciously on Aileen Fentamiglia. Alfred's mouth fell agape.

"Two trips," he fumbled out.

"Yes," said Aileen with increased emphasis, "and this is his third. To be exact, it's his second out of New York."

"Three trips," echoed Alfred Hibble rather foolishly.

"This boat-disease seems to be chronic in him, don't you think?"

"It beats everything," Alfred murmured.

"Sounds loony," continued Mr. Butterworth. "Ought to be tied up—"

"Excuse me," said Alfred Hibble, stroking his chin in a puzzled fashion and slowly wetting his lips. He started to move away. "I think I'll go and tell my wife."

When Alfred was gone, Mr. Butterworth threw his cigar away and heaved himself in his deck-chair toward Aileen, who had settled back and closed her eyes against the relentless glare of the sun. Her right hand lay indolently along the arm of her chair. Mr. Butterworth casually touched it and then let his big palm close over her slender fingers.

"You're a peach, Scotty." He observed at last with a short self-satisfied laugh. "I guess you spoofed him that time."

VI

After dinner that same evening Aileen, accompanied by Walter Merrett, a young composer, evidently talented, stepped out of the lounge. Walter Merrett had lived in Paris for about five years, and he was returning to his favorite haunts and his many friends after a brief visit to his family in Philadelphia. Walter Merrett was going back to accept an organist's job which had been unexpectedly offered him by letter. He was to be first organist in the American Church on the South Bank.

But Walter Merrett — who was after all a cosmopolite; who had many friends in Rome, Vienna and Paris, and who was a modernist when it came to his own musical composition — had no part, could indeed have no part in the troubled inner world of Alexis Kogan. Alexis Kogan after twenty years of unremitting industry and shrewdness had suddenly made up his mind to give up business; to put his factory into the care of a soviet of faithful employees. Tired of making a profit out of buttons, he had — to the astonishment of his closest friends and also to the employees themselves — thrown up everything to satisfy a whim, or perhaps to take a much-needed vacation in Europe.

Aileen and Merrett had taken several turns around the promenade deck when suddenly they ran into the sinister dark figure, lean and gangling. Aileen started slightly and pressed Walter Merrett's arm. Walter stiffened and waited to see what was going to happen next.

It must have been (Aileen reflected at once, startled though she was) just like this that Mrs. Hibble found herself face to face with the socalled "ghost", the subject of so much animated gossip on board within the last twenty-four hours. Mrs. Hibble had screamed and fled — probably because she was alone on deck. In any case, she hadn't expected the tall man with the wedge-shaped head. Mrs. Hibble hadn't, to be sure, enjoyed the benefit of the numerous theories that had been so abundantly aired since her somewhat untoward adventure the night before.

Aileen thought: Here we are on the Mermantia in mid-ocean. Lovely placid sea all around us. Myriads of stars above. No plunge or roll of the ship. What a smooth crossing! Thank goodness, Butterworth's been side-tracked tonight. I am fairly sick of Rotary luncheons and farewell dinners. Walter Merrett's nice and harmless. Ah — what's that? The madman! Why does he startle us that way, just as he did Mrs. Hibble — the silly old thing — last night? He's crazy, this buttons fellow! Just off his head — — —

The tall figure stopped directly in front of them. It stood poised there, but evidently uneasy, as though it were being blocked in its passage against its will. In the shadow of the bulkhead, quite irritated by the pair that now barred its path, it careened against something invisible. Perhaps it was against something inward. Perhaps it was against the rising wind. Yes, the Mermantia seemed to be gathering speed; she seemed to be ploughing along faster now, at about twenty two or three knots an hour. The wind towered up and began to whistle in the rigging and around the funnels.

The man in front of them wore a fawn topcoat, and he seemed to be tugging, in his helplessness and chagrin, at the lapels.

Presently Walter Merrett said: "Aileen, hadn't we better go in now? The wind's got its back up, I'm afraid, and you're not half warm enough in that wrap."

They turned round. Mr. Butterworth loomed up right behind them, puffing at his cigar.

"Good evening," he said with biting emphasis in his urbane tone. "How d'you do," he tossed at the tall uneasy man, who was trying nervously to pass by them.

The man paused in his effort. He looked pathetically tired. Obviously there was something wistful and forlorn about him.

"It's a fine night," said Mr. Butterworth, planting himself in front of the other.

"Yes, it's — a fine night." The man's voice was, however, charged with a questioning precision. He was embarrassed.

There was a long silence. In despair the tall man clutched his topcoat with one hand, and with the other combed his gray hair with his fingers. The hair was long, soft and wavy.

"A bit windy," put in Mr. Butterworth. "Feeling any better today? I heard you were off your feet last night."

The tall man's mind seemed to wander off into vacuity. He lost his balance for a moment; but soon regained it and stared blankly ahead.

Behind Mr. Butterworth cowered the stout form of Alfred Hibble, who seemed to be trying to wriggle out of an embarrassing dilemma; but nobody knew how he had got there. Alfred, half retreating now, watched the tall man's lips.

In a relentless tone, ignoring the other members of the little group, Mr. Butterworth inquired acidly: "Your name is Kogan, isn't it?"

"Yes," came the hoarse reply, bandied by the wind.

"Mine's Butterworth. Come on in and have a drink."

The tall man lowered his handsome head like a goaded bull ready to plunge.

"Thanks," he mumbled at last." I'm — — — not allowed to drink. On the wagon now. I'm under doctor's orders, you see —"

"Is that so?" Mr. Butterworth was overflowing with irony. "Well, if I were you," he added mock-sympathetically, "I'd button up that topcoat. The wind's coming up pretty sharp tonight, eh?"

The tall man obediently drew the fawn coat tighter about his elongated bony frame. After another uncertain pause, he sketched a gesture that was more than half a plea that he be allowed to pass and go on his way.

"Well, I'll be . . . ." burst involuntarily from Mr. Butterworth. "Why, man, you haven't got a single button on your coat. Now that's very queer — — — very queer — — —"

Alfred started to run away sidewise; but Mr. Butterworth seized his hand and kept him there by force. Walter Merrett felt Aileen shiver against his side. the tall man once more ran his hand through his gentle wavy hair, tousled by the wind.

"Where are your buttons, man?" persisted Mr. Butterworth, looking toward the others for approval.

"I guess — — I guess I must — — have lost them — — somewhere — —" Alexis Kogan stammered, seeking some loophole of escape.

"Lost them!" laughed Mr. Butterworth. "Now that's good. Very good. Tell us another. You don't expect us to believe that, do you? Be reasonable, man. He's lost them. Do you hear that?"

"Very queer," murmured Alfred Hibble, standing on one side.

"How could you lose them," continued Mr. Butterworth with

ruthless firmness, "unless you been through a laundry mangle?"

Aileen stepped forward as if she were bent on saving the tall man from further torment at the hands of the doorknob manufacturer from Seattle. She wished to reassure him, to say something consoling; but she couldn't find the necessary words.

Mr. Butterworth went on: "Did you pull them off yourself?"

"Perhaps I did. I — — — I don't seem to remember."

"Does this queer thing happen often to your — buttons?"

"I don't know." He paused like an animal at bay. Presently in a low mild voice, as if he were imploring pardon for some breach of taste or conduct, he added: "You see, I'm a bit absent-minded. And — that may account for it, though I'm not sure. I think I may have done it. The doctor's warned me. I must live a quiet regular life. Not that I've been irregular. No, that isn't it? Well, it's strange: I hear music at night. I've been hearing more and more of late — wild gypsy music, you know. And I can't sleep a wink. That's how it's been in recent years. I suppose I might very well have pulled off the buttons — — —"

"Weren't you a button-manufacturer once?" cut in Mr. Butterworth.

"Why, yes. I gave up business to go to Europe. I handed the business over to my employees. I think I told this lady, Madame Fenta — — — I think I told her about myself the first day out."

"You started to, Mr. Kogan, but you never finished. You told me you were on your way to visit your aged parents in Poland or somewhere."

"Look here, Kogan," burst impatiently from Mr. Butterworth, "it was you who scared Mrs. Hibble out of her wits last night. It *was* you. No use denying it. You might just as well own up —"

"I don't know," returned the tall man, lowering his head again, a tangled expression of pain about his mild eyes. He reached out his hand and supported himself against the shiny-white bulkhead. "Did I really do that? Did I? I'm very absent-minded."

"You needn't scare people, even if you're absent-minded," Mr. Butterworth insisted.

"If I frightened the lady, I apologize. I regret it. I'll explain to her. Will you not tell her I'm terribly sorry? Maybe I can make up for it. Music, perhaps. I dream about it all the time. I used to play the violin myself, just a bit. Does she like Beethoven, Mozart, Rimski-Korsakoff? It's an old story. Yes, I used to play." He made a faint motion of drawing a bow across the strings. "I don't play what you'd call well. I'm no maestro. No! That's the pity of it. . . . . But once . . . . oh, it was different, all right. I mean, when I first came to America.

183

About twenty five years ago. I wasn't a button manufacturer then. Of course not." He laughed as if to himself. "I was a musician. A young fiddler. But — that's an old story. I don't like much to speak of it . . . .

"Well, even if I say it myself now, I had rather a big future as a violinist. Anyway, that's what they all said in my home town . . . . I needn't bring that up now . . . . But I don't mind getting out my violin and playing for you. Just for you. I want the lady to be present, the lady I unintentionally frightened.

"After all these years, I am hoping it won't sound too bad either. Yes, Countess, I'm going to visit my old father and mother. Fact is, they think of me still as a fine musician. That's why I went to America twenty five years ago . . . . they're simple ignorant people. Just simple and ignorant. They think I'm a musician still, only a bigger and better one. They've never been to America, you see . . . . To them I'm moving from one glorious triumph to another, in Chicago, San Francisco, St. Louis, New Orleans . . . . everywhere. And I'm being acclaimed. I laugh a good deal, when I'm alone, at the fantastic idea. It really is a good joke on them — an excellent joke — I never told them about my success in the button business."

He laughed bitterly; and then went on: "I made money in buttons, though. I've fooled them all these years."

"What's your idea in not getting off the boat?" asked Walter Merrett.

"Oh, you've heard of that too. I suppose the stewards have told you, although I asked them to keep it a secret. Well, you see, I hate to land. I hate to take the train to Berlin, then to Warsaw, then to — — — How can I confess the truth to my people? I'm a musician, you see, and not a successful button-manufacturer. But this time I've made up my mind. I'm going ashore. I've gotten over my cowardice."

"That's right," commented Mr. Butterworth. "After all, you're a success and not a failure. The folks at home ought to be proud of you. Buck up, old man."

Kogan stared unseeingly at Mr. Butterworth, but he said nothing more. A profound silence had fallen on the little group surrounding the tall gangling man with the wedge-shaped head and the wavy grayish hair.

After a while Alfred Hibble in a shy misty voice broke the silence.

"Excuse me, everybody," he said, "but I must go and tell my wife."

R. G. G. Price
Maiden Voyage 1967

DAY II: The worst weather I remember. How dull the grey leaden waters are. Thank heavens I found I knew more about boat-building than I thought I did. Nasty quarrel at my table at dinner between my wife and Shem over Eve. The boy thinks she was a family asset, an ancestress to be proud of, while his mother says it is all because of her we are sailing about in cramped conditions instead of lolling in the Garden of Eden.

Day VII: Japheth has invented a curious sport: a ring of stiff rope is tossed across a string in accordance with elaborate rules. My wife has been busy milking Zebra. I never realised before how many of the beasts of the field supplied this compact nourishment. In the evening, Shem insisted on having what he called a "Séance." He prised a jewel out of Toad's head and foretold the most peculiar things, for example that a descendant of ours would be turned into a pillar of salt, no doubt for the best of reasons. Another thing was that greater arks than ours would sail and carry so many mariners that some would be spared from navigating to organise merriment. His last prediction was that, once men learn to avoid flood by voyaging through the air, it would become unlawful to travel with pets.

Day XVII: Nothing much to do but enjoy wine. Japheth says the cellar is getting low. Ham keeps walking round and round the deck, though I have warned him it will only increase his appetite.

Day XXIII: Nasty scene this morning between Giraffe and Ichneumon. How ever did Adam think up such unpronounceable names? The Serpent must have been active in the Garden long before he steered poor Eve into illicit fruit-picking. The Ark, which always did roll, has begun to pitch. This is having the most curious effect on Rabbit. Wonder what today's run is, if any?

Day XXIX: Shem keeps nagging me to have a boat drill but there doesn't seem much point as I didn't have time to make boats.

Day XXXIV: My birthday. For a surprise, the boys had made stringed instruments. I had been wondering where Cat had got to. After dinner they performed waltzes and selections from operettas. Keel slightly stove in by some large sea creature. There certainly isn't any decline in *marine* fauna. Bee swarming on poop.

Day XXXIX: Decided to use Dove as lookout. Shem says she's too stupid and wants me to send Buzzard. The great advantage of Dove is her docility. If I tell her to come back, she will come back. I have never felt at ease with Buzzard. He gives me the absurd feeling I'm to blame for all the leaks.

Day LII: I had somehow got it into my mind we were going to make landfall in forty days. My wife is dissatisfied with her cabin.

Day LXX: Is there anything more boring than a long voyage with the same people at your table for every meal?

Day CVIII: Seen my first liger.

Day CXV: I am getting angry with Japheth's moans about the shortage of girls. Why can't he take an interest in nature? If he wants exercise, he can always join Ham or go for a swim.

Day CXXX: My wife has decided it's time we redecorated and spends all day designing. I'm afraid she wants to use some of the passengers' skins.

Day CXXXV: I am thinking of sending Dove out again, in spite of Shem's sneers. He has worked out some kind of test of intelligence and Dove rates low. Ham says the shape of the Ark is all wrong and that's why it always seems to be going sideways.

Day CXL: Dove has returned with a beakfull of seaweed. Shem may not look clever but he has flair.

Day CXLIX: How can we have a sweep on the day's run when we keep floating on and off reefs? Dove has turned up with a branch that Ham says may be olive, the tree that produces those little green savoury fruits. Why can't she find some vine leaves?

Day CL: We've grounded. Japheth wants to sit tight and wait till we float off and land in some delta with lots of seafood and music and girls; but the rest of the family say they're bored with my Ark and can't wait till they're squelching about on dry land. I warned them that all they'd be able to do would be to grow rice. At least we shall be able to kick the animals out soon. They have been pampered far too long and look spoiled. This should be our last evening so my wife says we must dine in fancy-dress.

Day CLI: And now we've got to climb Mount Ararat *downwards!*

Michael A. Musmanno
Bed and Breakfast 1958

A YEAR had passed since a ship had sailed from New York Harbor carrying a youthful passenger who, sick at heart and a little confused, hoped to find among the ancient ruins of the Old World the balm of Gilead for hurts and bruises received in the New World. His wounds now healed, the voyager yearned for home like a runaway boy who (contrary to his expectations) finds that his absence has not been mourned.

Although the S.S. *Leviathan* on which I was scheduled to leave was not due to sail from Southampton until seven o'clock on a Tuesday evening, I came dashing across the pier at seven o'clock that morning. The ship's officer at the gangplank held up his hand. "Just a moment. You've made a mistake. The ship sails at seven this evening."

I replied: "I made no mistake. I want to go aboard now."

He elucidated further: "You would find it very dull aboard, sir. The salons are closed, the musicians have not arrived, the shuffle-board courts are not ready —"

I broke in: "But are they serving meals?"

"Oh yes, you can have your meals."

"That's all I want to know." And I scurried up the gangplank faster than a war refugee. When I had arrived in London a week before, I had only enough money to pay for lodging. Fortunately, in many hostelries in London breakfast is included in the price of lodging, and the combination is known as "bed and breakfast." Thus, each morning before setting off for the courts I filled up on the traditional British breakfast of bacon, eggs, muffins, jams, toast, and coffee, which constituted my fare for the day. But no matter how much youth consumes for breakfast he wants lunch and dinner as well. So on the morning of the sailing I felt within me the ravenous cumulative appetite of seven unappeased lunches and dinners.

In all the history of good eating, not even King Henry VIII feasted more felicitously than I did during that five-day journey between Southampton and New York. At seven-thirty each morning fruit juice and black coffee appeared like magic in my stateroom. At eight-thirty, in the ship's dining room, I attacked a matinal repast of cereal, eggs, bacon, potatoes, and hot cakes. At noontime the table glowed, smiled, and chuckled with soup, steak, vegetables, salad, dessert, and coffee. At four o'clock tea, little sandwiches and cakes refreshed the oceanic afternoon, and at seven each evening a royal banquet unfolded in the large dining hall where one's eyes dilated as his belt yielded to appetizers, smoked oysters, celery, soup, roast fowl, vegetables, salad, nuts, fruit, pie, ice cream, and demitasse. At 10 P.M. — I skipped the chafing-dish supper available to those trenchermen who had capacity for it.

The voyage added nine pounds to my sparse frame. From the day I had left New York I had been living, not exactly on Oliver Twist rations, but far from what a healthy young man of twenty-six liked to have. My employment on the Continent hardly ever provided compensation commensurate with the human interest it afforded. There was the time that the *centesimi* and the half-lira coins in my pocket produced only enough of a jingle to call to my pantry box a large bag of black olives and two loaves of bread. With these provisions I held the fort for four days until a check arrived from the Florentine publisher. I have not been able to look at a black olive since. Not long ago I related this four-day olive story to a lady, expecting that the termination of my narrative would draw from her an expression of amused sympathy over my melancholy siege. I was considerably astonished, however, when she remarked: "You certainly were lucky! I just adore black olives!"

The voyage was an Odyssey of enchantment. I ate and slept better than any of the monarchs and princes of old whose castles I had visited in Europe, and I was returning to the greatest land in the world — to embrace again my sweetheart. How could one be happier? Not the slightest doubt entered my mind that Miss Law awaited me eagerly and that we would celebrate a felicitous reconciliation.

Aboard the *Leviathan* I achieved a rather unique fame, in no way associated with the law. Before leaving Rome I had sent my trunk ahead with directions that it be placed aboard the ship at Cherbourg, the eastern terminus of her run. Boarding the vessel at Southampton, I was informed my trunk could not be found. On the possibility that it might have been delivered to the wrong cabin, the purser allowed me to inspect the ship from stern to stern and to visit any cabin to look for the missing luggage. In this search I came into contact with practically every passenger and member of the crew, and I soon became known as "the young man who lost his trunk." Then it developed that Nazimova, the celebrated stage and screen star, also making the passage, had similarly lost her trunk, so we became the team of "Nazimova and Musmanno, the two who lost their trunks!"

Happily I looked forward to the moment when the great tragedienne would locate her missing property or become convinced it had been irretrievably lost. Inevitably she would hurl herself into a dramatic outburst worthy of her superb histrionic talents. For the time I forgot all about my own straying baggage and hugged myself in anticipatory glee as I visualized the dramatic treat of the century when Nazimova should emote over her wandering hatbox and mysteriously vanished trunk. But a desolate disillusionment ensued. When her luggage showed up on the Hoboken pier she merely shrugged a casual hip and remarked: "Well, it's about time."

My own trunk still played hide-and-seek. However, two months later it unobtrusively arrived at my home. I learned subsequently that it had been placed on the wrong ship, followed Columbus' route to the West Indies, returned to Cherbourg, and finally limped into Stowe Township, worn and battered but with its cargo safe.

But a more resplendent title awaited me than the one which identified me, as the traveler without a trunk. Aside from the time which I spent in the various dining rooms, which I admit was not inconsiderable, I devoted all my waking hours to working on a series of articles entitled "A Philadelphia Lawyer in the European Courts" for possible publication in legal journals at home. To the other passengers I must have seemed the proverbial bookworm. I never carried less than a half dozen books under my arms; I was constantly dropping papers and pencils which, as I walked, I stooped to pick up, only to lose a book or a pen or two. My fingers revealed telltale inkstains, my wearing apparel was indifferent, my hair was combed by the winds. I participated in none of the deck social life and engaged in no general conversation. I was a recluse and continued to be known as "the young man who lost his trunk."

One day while slouched studiously in my steamer chair surrounded by numerous tomes and notebooks, I overheard two fellow voyagers animatedly discussing the athletic contest scheduled for the ship's passengers when we should arrive in mid-Atlantic. Each of the two men was choosing a team of ten persons, the resulting teams to compete against each other on an individual as well as collective basis. It seemed they had already collected eighteen contestants, and each leader needed one more to complete his squad of athletes. One of the captains said: "Why don't you take the young fellow who lost his trunk?" and he pointed a casual finger in my direction. I did not lift my head but tensed a curious and windward ear. The other captain said: "What? Him? He wouldn't know a shuffleboard from a hundred-yard dash. All he knows is books, books, books."

The first captain rejoined: "Well, we've searched the ship over and he and that fellow from Cincinnati are the only ones left who could possibly qualify on weight. Suppose you take the 'trunk man' and I'll take the guy from Cincinnati."

"Oh no, you don't," the second captain flung back almost indignantly. "That's not fair. The Cincinnati fellow at least occasionally takes a hike around the deck. I'll tell you what we'll do. We'll toss a coin, and the man who wins takes Cincinnati, the one who loses takes the 'trunk guy'; that is, if we can get him away from his traveling library."

Thus was I shanghaied into the oceanic olympiad that memorable summer of 1925. The competitive sports included running, jumping, wrestling, swimming, and shuffleboard, which I had never played before. In view of the conversation I had overheard, I determined that I would show the team captains how wrong they were on the subject of my athletic capacity. I hurled myself into the games with the vigor and resolution of one fighting for his very life. Our team won the most collective points. That evening, however, I could not move a limb, and dinner was served to me in my cabin. Nor did any power of locomotion return to me the following day. Confined to my berth as I was, every muscle in my body protested and lamented, as must have protested and lamented the muscles of that turtle which beat the rabbit. On the eve of our arrival in New York, prizes were awarded at the final and farewell dinner. Several members of my team practically carried me hammock-fashion to the banquet hall and there I was decorated with a medal which proclaimed me "The Mid-Atlantic Athletic Champion."

I highly treasure that disk of bronze which today has its place among its more austere brothers awarded during the war. The latter ones may have been gained at more risk of life and limb, but certainly not with any more win-or-die effort.

Ever since that wondrous voyage I have cherished a deep affection for the *Leviathan*. Prior to World War I, when she was the Hamburg-American liner *Vaterland,* she plied between French and English ports and New York, the largest passenger ship afloat. In 1914, at the outbreak of war, she was interned and then, in 1917, when the United States entered the conflict, she was taken as enemy property, converted into a troop-carrying vessel, and during the next two years ferried 240,000 troops across the Atlantic. Following World War I she was sold to the United States Lines and returned to the trans-Atlantic passenger service, and while in that service I became probably her happiest passenger.

Good old United States Ship *Leviathan*. When at last she became too old for active service and lay rusting at her pier in Hoboken, I never failed to visit her when I chanced to be in New York. In the end she was sold to a commercial firm in China, to haul sand, gravel, and scrap iron. I read this account in the newspapers, and as I did so I visualized with a melancholy heart that magnificent mistress of the yeasty deep now degraded to the menial tasks of a harbor scow. As I thought of her departing forever from the frothy American lanes over which she had long been queen, a knot formed in my throat and, taking out the medal I had won on her gleaming decks, a tear obscured but did not completely hide the fact that once, in my book-inundated life, I was the "Mid-Atlantic Athletic Champion."

Loving The Sea

*S*itting on a seachest and swaying
to and fro..., I began to consider
whether it was only the books about the
sea which I had loved hitherto, and not the
sea itself. Perhaps it is better not to live
with it, if you would love it. The sea is at
its best at London, near midnight, when
you are within the arms of a capacious
chair, before a glowing fire, selecting
phases of the voyages you will never make.
It is wiser not to try to realize your dreams.
There are no real dreams.
— *H. M. Tomlinson, 1912.*

FELLOW CITIZENS

The Customs

❧Return

❧*Arriving home can be almost as fun as going away, especially if you forget about all the work awaiting you, and the demands: the house, the kids, the parents, the pets. If you don't, you'll end up feeling like Mark Twain when he came back from a long Pacific cruise:*

> *Aug. 13. San Francisco. Home again. No not home again - in prison again and all the wide sense of freedom gone. The city seems so cramped and so dreary with toil and care and business anxiety. God help me, I wish I were at sea again.*

If this makes you the least bit hesitant to go on a cruise, since you will have to return, let S. J. Perelman set you right.

S. J. Perelman
Oh, You're Back 1947

THE arrival of the *Queen Mary* in New York, far from being the noisy, vivid pageant we expected, was as fleeting and elusive as an episode in a Kafka novel. Stealthily, almost as if fate begrudged us the satisfaction of seeing the harbor and the skyline, we were wafted from the open sea one evening to a North River pier the following dawn. The whole process was a grotesque mixture of the ephemeral and the banal; we descended the gangplank with no more illusion of having spanned the Atlantic than though we had commuted from Weehawken. It was only when our consorts and the fledglings streamed toward us from behind the barrier that our bewilderment abated. To say it disappeared entirely would be untrue; at one point in the resulting scrimmage, I discovered myself bussing a willowy showgirl under the impression that she was Hirschfeld's infant daughter, at another I was dandling a peppery old gentleman on my knee and quizzing him about his progress at school. At last, however, we managed to unsnarl our respective kinfolk, and after a breathless résumé of the fire, flood, and famine that had occurred in our absence, plunged into the ordeal of the customs examination.

Three quarters of an hour afterward, a fetching tableau might have presented itself to anyone sufficiently curious to invade the section bearing my initial. Knee-deep in a mound of shawls, brocades, bracelets, necklaces, purses, fans, and bric-a-brac resembling the contents of a thrift shop, three nonplused inspectors were attempting to calculate the duty I owed. My wife and I, our faces drawn, sat on the sidelines tonelessly discussing some practical solution to the dilemma — flight, a rubber check, a fifth mortgage on our home, selling the children. Under the circumstances, the last seemed the most feasible, inasmuch as they were loading the antique pistols I had bought them with percussion caps and discharging them into our eardrums. I am still not sure how I ever got off the hook, except that a few weeks afterward Hirschfeld showed me an I.O.U. with my name signed in a shaky scrawl. It was, needless to say, a blatant forgery and beneath contempt, but rather than see my friend victimized by some unscrupulous rascal, I shouldered the responsibility and settled with him for ten cents on the dollar.

Speeding across town from the pier to the family flat, I was dismayed to find hardly any civic recognition of our return; no bunting decked the buildings, almost no crowds clustered about the cab showering it with confetti and cheering hoarsely, and a minimum of brass bands lined the sidewalk before my residence. The sole member of the welcoming committee, a beery doorman chewing a half-dead cigar stump, eyed me with restrained enthusiasm as I sprang from the taxi. "Oh, *you're* back, are you?" he commented sourly. "Well, won't be long before I'll be carrying *you* upstairs four o'clock in the morning."

A similarly fervent salutation greeted me on entering our front door. The woolly little puppy I remembered cuddling in my arms, now grown to mastiff proportions, took one rapid sniff and zestfully sank his fangs into my ankle. By stroking him gently on the head with a length of chain, though, I won his confidence, and, dusting glass and shredded wallpaper from my shoulders, groped my way into the nest. Nothing was changed; the veneer on our installment furniture curled as crazily as ever and a disgruntled maid (not the one I recalled, but another equally morose) was stuffing herself with caviar and watering the whiskey. Subsequently I observed her comparing me furtively with my photograph on the piano and shaking her head. "Don't try and tell *me* that's the same man," I overheard her declaring to the broom. Whoever I was, she obviously thought me worthy of respect, because from then on she seldom ventured into my presence without a bread-knife concealed under her apron.

❧*Most of the fun in coming home is in plaguing your family and friends with stories about all the things you saw and all the places you visited, and they haven't (for an expertly rhymed version of the friend's point of view, see the final selection, a poem by Ogden Nash). You earn their patience in listening to you or watching your slides by bringing them exotic presents from exotic lands, things they'll never use, like ginger soap and conch jewelry. If they don't like the presents enough, however, beware: they might ask you questions and give you their opinions, which might make the whole trip seem not only far away, but worthless. And then, as in D. Keith Mano's piece, there are mothers.*

E. W. Howe
Just to Please the Neighbors 1927

THE Missourian who is not having a good time, and who yesterday wrote a complaint to the St. Louis *Globe-Democrat,* occupies a room across the hall from mine, and he frequently comes in to grumble. He leaves the "Simla" at Singapore, and goes to Batavia.

"I don't want to go to Batavia," he said to me this morning, "but if I don't go, when I return home people will say I missed the best thing out here. So I am going to Batavia, although I know nothing about it, care nothing about it, and hate the name of it. I came on this trip, anyway, just to please the neighbors. They kept telling me of the delights of foreign travel and here I am, as miserable as I can be."

When I return home I shall pretend to have visited every town and country, not because I shall enjoy the reputation of being a great traveler, but as a protection. I have observed that when you have failed to visit a certain place, other travelers say you "missed it," and that the places you did visit are visited by everybody, and do not amount to much. In addition to this, I shall invent places of interest, and claim to have visited them. I resolved to do this at Kyoto, and asked forgiveness of the thousand images in one of the temples. If silence gives consent, it is all right with the images.

D. Keith Mano
My Mother Doesn't Go to Haiti 1979

"Hello?"

"It's me."

"Mother. How was the cruise?"

"Don't ask."

"I won't."

"You don't care to know how your mother suffered?"

"I'll ask."

"At least the *Titanic* had decency enough to sink itself. Hours we stood in San Juan waiting to get on board. I've seen pictures of Ellis Island in 1905: same set-up, but not 97 degrees all the time. Then we couldn't find the right cabin. The travel agent warned me — he should sink, too — Cunard never presses down hard enough on a ballpoint pen. No one could read the stateroom number on the carbon copy. But that's the British: so veddy genteel they wouldn't push on a ballpoint pen too hard.

"Deluxe this was. Two beds, each with an iron rail six inches high around: like we were in intensive care. You know my condition, I have to get up three, four times a night — what was I going to do, pole-vault out in pitch blackness? So I call the steward and he asks, 'Are you in an upper bunk?' That's deluxe. With undeluxe you also have to vault six feet to the floor. Not one place to sit: it was either on the intensive care rail or on the toilet. Worse, the air conditioning was so glacial, if you died, your body would keep until the boat got back to Puerto Rico. No adjustment knob except, just where it was handiest, in the middle of the ceiling. Your poor sister had to make a staircase out of the bureau drawers and climb up to move it from COMFORT — COMFORT for a popsicle — to OFF. Which should have read DEATH, because in five minutes the room was a floating can of Sterno."

"Was Caracas nice at least?"

"How should I know? The boat was too weak to get there: only three propellers propelled or something. So they threw in an extra island. Why not? You can't tell them apart anyway. For my money — which was considerable — we could've been landing on the same island all week. Pay $25 and they wedge you into the same excursion bus, with the same seats for someone without a coccyx bone. You drive through the same fruit grove up a mountain — and what do they show you? Your own miserable, underpropelled boat down below. At least I thought I'd get an authentic fruit drink. A dollar fifty I shelled out, to watch a man open a gallon can of Bluebird orange juice."

"But Barbados — ?"

"Like Coney Island with bananas. In 1968 it was nice — a beautiful beach. Now they've extended the hotel out so far there's eight inches of sand left. I put down my blanket, took off my shoes, and — whoosh — a big wave came in and filled my pocketbook with seaweed. Everything wet: soaked me like my travel agent did."

"Uh. The food?"

"Lots of it, mostly dinosaur meat. Sixteen courses — racecourses, if you're in the first sitting. The waiter has to shove you out quick before the next bunch comes. It's like a 78 rpm revolving smorgasbord. And rough: who says the Caribbean is serene? First night I feel like I'm walking on Saturn, lead orthopedic shoes. The waiter says we're going upstream. Two nights later I'm on the moon, bouncing. We're headed downstream, he says. Nobody tells you beforehand, there's this crazy escalator in the middle of the Caribbean."

"So where are you now? At the Sans Souci in Miami?"

"Ha. My travel agent: he couldn't book you from Times Square to Grand Central. I debark in San Juan, lugging my own luggage — after my recent operation, my more recent fractured hand, and my present terrible headcold from too much COMFORT — Cunard wouldn't distress a ballpoint pen, but a crippled woman is a burro to them — in San Juan and no plane to Miami. At last Eastern decides we can hop a flight that'll make just one stop — in Haiti. So we stand on line for two hours behind ten dozen Haitians with great baskets of fruit and produce, every pineapple of which has to be examined in case it's a hand grenade. Finally we get to the counter and — ho — it seems that if your sister has no birth certificate she can land in Haiti, but she can never leave again. Marjorie, I say, you are not going to look good with a basket of mangos on your head from here to eternity. I panicked. Eastern panicked. 'Run!' they yell. 'Go stop your luggage!' And there I am, racing out on the runway, under airplanes, looking through six thousand suitcases and crates of papaya. No luggage."

"You mean — ?"

"Don't interrupt, it gets worse. By luck I crawl to Miami flying standby. Three hours later the banana plane from Haiti arrives: nothing. My headstrong luggage is on vacation by itself in Port-au-Prince. Enough: I take a cab to the Sans Souci. You know why the Sans Souci is called the Sans Souci? Because it is C-L-O-S-E-D.

Maybe in chapter 11 even. I've been booked into a defunct hotel. It's me that has the *souci.*

"So I try the Eden Roc, which fortunately is about as busy as Pompeii in 80 A.D. They lodge me in the garret, where the roc used to nest when Miami was still fashionable. But how am I going to impress Eastern? Aha. I call and I tell the woman, 'Look — I had my hair in that suitcase.' After the seventh time, I hear a man say in the background, 'It's the bald woman calling again.' But it worked. After 48 hours my bags arrived and now I really have trouble."

"Why?"

"My clothes, I realize, are nothing to write to Haiti about. And they've been sat on by Port-au-Princeans for two days. How can I go any place? The people in the Eden Roc — all five of them — they'll say, '*That's* what she's been screaming about?' So right now I'm going down the back stairs to buy a complete new wardrobe. A fortune it'll cost. What does Eastern Airlines care about my pride?"

"Well —"

"How are things in New York?"

"Don't ask."

"I wasn't going to. Goodbye."

Ogden Nash
Marco Polo Notwithstanding 1931

> There are those who always select Cunarders to travel trans
> Atlanticly via,
> Perhaps because they are ocean greyhounds, perhaps
> because their names all end in -ia.
> Then there are those who prefer White Star liners on which
> to be well or sick,
> Perhaps because they too are ocean greyhounds, or perhaps
> because their names all end in -ic.
> There are others who prefer the French Line or the North
> German Lloyd
> Or a dozen different lines which specialize in taking people
> abroyd.
> As for myself, like most of my ilk I haven't sufficient
> revenue
> To get very far from 38th Street and Medison Evenue.
> I have never paced a deck looking nautically to windward
> and leeward,

Or sat between two bores at the captain's table or
    requested a receptacle of the steward
And when I get in travelled company I feel very American
    and provincial
And try to pass it all off with some jest borrowed from the
    column of Walter Winciall
But there is no stoplight
For a talkative cosmoplite.
They are as repetitious and prolix
As confirmed alcoholix
And will insist on describing in many badly chosen words
    to any unfortunate godforsaken hearer
The delights of London and Vienna and Paris and the
    Rivearer
And the low cost of living and the incredible politeness of
    the servants
And Prohibition's universal unobservants
And a lot of other little points they have picked up in their
    voyaging,
And altogether they manage to be pretty damned
    annoyaging.
Oh Lord;
Why doesn't everybody that goes abrord stay abrord?

❧ *Well, it's time to disembark, to go down that humorous gangway
and back to the real, serious world. All ashore, final port o' call, drop
anchor, mark twain, land the lubbers at last. On behalf of all the
humorists, travel writers, and cartoonists who have laughed at the sea
and all the things bold or silly enough to think they can try to walk or
otherwise find a way across it, I wish you* bon voyage.

Acknowledgments

PETER ARNO: Reprinted from *Peter Arno,* Dodd, Mead, © 1979, by permission of the estate of the artist. LUDWIG BEMELMANS: Reprinted by permission of International Creative Management. ROBERT C. BENCHLEY: "Seeing Off" and "What to Read at Sea — If Anything" from *The Treasurer's Report and Other Aspects of Community Singing* by Robert C. Benchley. Copyright 1930 by Robert C. Benchley. Renewed 1958 by Gertrude D. Benchley. "Traveling in Peace" from *Inside Benchley* by Robert C. Benchley. Copyright 1925 by Harper & Row, Publishers, Inc. Renewed 1953 by Gertrude D. Benchley. Both reprinted by permission of Harper & Row, Publishers, Inc. NICHOLAS COLERIDGE: Reprinted from *Around the World in 78 Days,* McGraw-Hill, © 1985, by permission of the publisher. CLARENCE DAY: Reprinted by permission; © 1934, 1962 The New Yorker Magazine, Inc. DONEGAN: Both reproduced by permission of *Punch.* COREY FORD: Reprinted by permission of Harold Ober Associates Incorporated. Copyright 1929 by Corey Ford. HENNING GENTRIIS: Reproduced by permission of *Punch.* WOLCOTT GIBBS: Reprinted by permission of Dodd, Mead & Company, Inc. from *Bed of Neuroses* by Wolcott Gibbs. Copyright 1937 by Wolcott Gibbs. Copyright renewed 1965 by Wolcott Gibbs, Jr. and Janet Ward. RUBE GOLDBERG AND SAM BOAL: Reprinted from *Rube Goldberg's Guide to Europe* by Rube Goldberg and Sam Boal, by permission of Vanguard Press, Inc. Copyright © 1954, by Rube Goldberg and Sam Boal. Renewed © 1982 by Irma Goldberg and Sam Boal. RICHARD GORDON: © 1967 Richard Gordon, by permission of Curtis Brown. ARTHUR GUITERMAN: Reprinted by permission; © 1933, 1961 The New Yorker Magazine Inc. MERRILY HARPUR: Reproduced by permission of *Punch.* PHYLLIS HARTNOLL: Reproduced by permission of *Punch.* MARK KELLEY: Drawing by Kelley; © 1925, 1953 The New Yorker Magazine, Inc. JEAN KERR: From *Penny Candy* by Jean Kerr. Copyright © 1966, 1967, 1968, 1969, 1970 by Collins Productions, Inc. Reprinted by permission of Doubleday, a division of Bantam, Doubleday, Dell Publishing Group, Inc. ANATOL KOVARSKY: Reprinted from Anatol Kovarsky, *Kovarsky's World,* © 1956, by permission of the artist. LAWRENCE LARIAR: Reprinted from *Happy Holiday,* Dodd, Mead, © 1956, by permission of the publisher. STEPHEN LONGSTREET: Copyright by Stephen Longstreet renewed 1970. Reprinted by permission of the author. PIERRE LOVING: Reprinted from *Americans Abroad: An Anthology,* ed. Peter Neagoe, Servire Press, 1932, by permission of the publisher. PHYLLIS McGINLEY: "Cruise Captain's Chantey" reprinted from *One More Manhattan,* Harcourt, Brace, © 1937, by permission of Patsy Blake. "The Sea Chantey Around Us" from *Times Three* by Phyllis McGinley.

3⁰⁰   Gen 1/15 TD